Barnes & Noble Critical Studies

General Editor: Anne Smith

James Purdy

JAMES PURDY

Stephen D. Adams

BARNES & NOBLE
BOOKS
10 East 53d St., New York 10022
(a division of Harper & Row Publishers. Inc.)

Barnes & Noble Books
Harper & Row, Publishers, Inc.
10 East 53rd Street
New York

ISBN 0–06–490014–2

LC 76–40878

**For Mike,
and for Josiane**

First published in the U.S.A. 1976

Printed and bound in Great Britain
MCMLXXVI

Contents

Acknowledgements

Grateful thanks are due to James Purdy, his agents David Higham Associates Ltd, and the following publishers for permission to reprint copyright material:

Excerpts from *Color of Darkness*, copyright © 1956, 1957 by James Purdy; excerpts from *Children is All*, copyright © 1957, 1959, 1960, 1961 by James Purdy; reprinted by permission of New Directions Publishing Corporation.

Excerpts from *Malcolm*, copyright © 1959 by James Purdy; excerpts from *The Nephew*, copyright © 1960 by James Purdy; excerpts from *Cabot Wright Begins*, copyright © 1964 by James Purdy; excerpts from *Eustace Chisholm and the Works*, copyright © 1967 by James Purdy; reprinted by permission of Farrar, Straus & Giroux, Inc.

Excerpts from *Jeremy's Version*, copyright © 1970 by James Purdy; excerpts from *I am Elijah Thrush*, copyright © 1972 by James Purdy, copyright © 1971 by Esquire, Inc.; excerpts from *The House of the Solitary Maggot*, copyright © 1974 by James Purdy; reprinted by permission of Doubleday & Company, Inc.

Excerpts from *In a Shallow Grave*, copyright © 1976 by James Purdy; reprinted with the permission of Arbor House Publishing Company.

I should also like to thank Judy Jacques for her patient criticism and support.

Introduction

This book seeks to define the steady progress of Purdy's art and to explore his evolving themes and preoccupations. Although he has been widely acclaimed as one of America's major contemporary writers there is as yet no clear consensus of opinion with regard to the nature of his fiction. The primary intention, then, is to provide an account of that unfolding imagination, by a close reading of his work. Whilst the author's affinities with other writers are noted, the emphasis of this study is upon the individual and distinctive qualities of his vision and there is no systematic comparison of his achievement with the whole range of present-day American novelists.* Nonetheless, it would seem appropriate to make some prefatory remarks on the diversity of reaction his work has provoked and to give an outline of the alternative viewpoint that is to be argued.

Purdy's literary career suggests the struggle of a dissenting individual voice to break through patterns of conformity. The earliest work was printed privately by friends and he was first published commercially in England. Though championed by writers such as Dame Edith Sitwell and John Cowper Powys, Purdy has never enjoyed the support or approval of the American literary establishment. Admittedly, when his work began to appear in the late fifties, its highly wrought style and proliferation of bizarre characters might have been expected to disturb popular critics who had

---

* Although I disagree with some of the provisional assessments in the chapter 'Frames Without Pictures' which discusses Purdy's earlier fiction, I have great respect for Tony Tanner's survey of American literature from 1950 to 1970, City of Words, (Jonathan Cape, 1971) and would refer readers interested in comparative criticism to this seminal work.

7

ordained a diet of representational social realism with its 'instant relevance'. Those prescriptions that had so singularly failed to quell Faulkner's 'heresies' in earlier decades lingered on. Despite the fact that the fifties and sixties were increasingly characterised by experimentation, the author tended to be frowned upon for what was often regarded as wilful eccentricity, for his apparent idiosyncrasies, his quirks and mannerisms of style. Even in the mid-sixties, faced with the complex satire of *Cabot Wright Begins*, there were still a few solemn edicts against those who had succumbed to a temptation to take Purdy seriously. Elsewhere, his growing reputation has been accounted for in terms of a vogue for 'black humour' or 'American gothic'. Others have been eager to claim or reject him as a 'gay writer' since homosexual love happens to be portrayed as openly as other forms and is accorded the same potency for redemption or perdition. Finally, a much subtler version of that doubt as to whether he could be fully conceded the stature of a serious artist has been expressed in the view that his work comes close to a self-consuming parody of the whole fiction-making process, a flirtation with literary suicide.

This study hopes to show that Purdy's originality and extraordinary talents cannot be neatly inventoried and that to portray him as the author of an eccentric body of fiction, as a part of some movement or fashionable literary trend, or as a novelist who essentially mocks the capacities of art, is to deny the complexities of his individual voice. His own description of his work as an exploration of the American soul conveyed in a style based on the rhythms and accents of American speech runs contrary to such categories and is a claim that merits examination.

The author's distinctive formal and philosophic preoccupations need to be seen in a broader, more tentative perspective. Although it has an urgent bearing upon the present day, there is a timeless quality to his work. The avowed concern for the world of the spirit and its relation to language evokes the native tradition of Melville and Hawthorne with their passion for metaphysics and command of symbolist techniques. As might be expected, there is also an evident fascination with the hellenic age when speculations on human destiny were at an intense pitch. Purdy sees modern America as the enemy of the soul and would subvert the suffocating patterns its culture imposes upon the individual self by his own

8

exemplary fictions. Thus his families and miniature societies are simultaneously the vehicles for an exploration of the national psyche. At another level he re-tells, in his own special idiom, the Christian story of how a being charged with life's spiritual or divine possibilities is denied kinship in the larger world. It is misleading, then, to insist on measuring the characters in such a drama by the criteria of social realism or by those of a strict psychological verisimilitude. They are projections of the inner life, put forward as hypotheses about existence and endowed with the reality of the author's innermost convictions. Regarded in this light, art is accorded the highest functions—it keeps alive the memory of those ingredients that have been excluded from everyday existences and Purdy might more profitably be seen as the 'memorialist' of the qualities that have gone missing from his native culture. He is the self-styled prophet and chronicler of its omissions.

The philosophic basis of his work might loosely be described as that of the Christian existentialist. The difficulty of the individual's quest for an authentic selfhood in a society whose commercial forces, in particular, are pitted in opposition, is imaged in that pervasive feeling of being all alone in an alien, absurd world. Characters are mysteriously orphaned and cut off from the source of their spiritual identity, in exile from some heavenly home. Their 'homelessness' is captured in those moments when the everyday fabric of life is suddenly shot through by radical doubt as they become aware of an essence that cannot be fulfilled within the terms of earthly existence. A typical reaction is to abdicate the painful struggle, to refuse to live in the present and to conjure up idealised realms within the past or future. Though Purdy is fond of alluding to Platonic doctrines to comment on these inner yearnings, he is also acutely aware of the dangers associated with attempts to arrest life in forms that simulate such ideals. His vision has affinities with that expounded by Unamuno in his book *The Tragic Sense of Life*, for both articulate in their different ways the sense that it is the dialectic of faith and doubt itself, with its roots in the paradox of suffering, that offers an authentic mode of being. This religious dimension is responsible for that elusive manner in which highly individualised characters seem inseparably involved in some mythological drama or mystery play, in which life discourses upon its own possibilities and failings. This is not to suggest we are presented with dimly veiled allegories, but that the author's focus is upon the minute interactions of different levels of being.

These interactions are communicated by subtle formal strategies as distinct layers or patterns of meaning are brought into contact. Purdy resembles Faulkner in the sheer quantity of narrators he employs. But now the narrative act has turned in upon itself and instead of dramatising a search for meaning, it more frequently exemplifies the author's notion that real life has been reduced to the texture of a fiction. His characters typically aspire to an omniscience over the raw materials of their destiny and of those around them. Yet the stultifying consequences of such attempts to superimpose a story upon the actual world of love and suffering are constantly exposed by the subversive artistry of Purdy himself. Their elaborate constructions are caused to perform a slow dance of death, to spell out the 'inside story' as we are brought to read 'between the lines'.

1

Early Stories and *Malcolm*

James Purdy has said he prefers not to give a biography since his biography is in his work. He avoids publicity and is reluctant to package his personality in the terminology of the media as if it were a commodity to be sold. This is bound up with a belief that the already problematic relationship between words and inner experience has been placed under acute pressure from the usurpation of language by commercial and other forces. It is apt to think of his work as an alternative form of biography. But rather than document the outward, visible contours of life, it develops a concern for and a revelation of identity at another level. There emerges the inner portrait of a man at odds with the processes of anaesthesia in his society, whose stories and novels focus upon the difficulties of communicating the spiritual self and of living, or writing, a 'real-life' history as opposed to a fiction of one's own or somebody else's composition. Moreover, the idea of the biography can be applied in a tentative sense to the overall direction of this body of work; it unfolds a collective record of the self's possibilities and constrictions in the various phases of existence brought about by the passage of time.

Since the author's early work abounds in images of the child, orphaned, abandoned, or the captive of a tyrannous love, the present chapter examines those stories that centre upon the relation to a father figure and the culmination of this theme in the first novel—*Malcolm*. The following chapter pursues the complementary images of mother and child and their bearing upon the second novel—*The Nephew*. The home, the starting point in this collective biography, is no longer the crucible of the emotional life. It is depicted as a place of darkness, at the heart of which the child

11

serves as the living memory of the self that has been forsaken. The title under which the first stories were eventually published, *Color of Darkness* (1957), suggests this 'underground' realm of spirit the author addresses himself to and the problematic necessity of having to use the very materials of expression which he senses are now antagonistic to his aims. Given his belief that language is no longer the vehicle of feeling in the larger world, he must, nonetheless, struggle to reclaim it for his own purposes. His provisional solution is to dramatise this paradox and to recreate the continual tensions between the inner life and the ability of words to communicate or falsify its nature. It leads him to organise the form of his fiction in an intricate fashion so that the speech his characters employ is refracted through a delicate lens of symbol and myth. Such an approach allows him to evoke the living tissue of felt experience from which the spoken word is frequently seen to have wrenched itself free.

The title story reveals the ingenuity with which the failure to know one's self or another person is shown to have its counterpart in a breakdown of language. It concerns a man's inability to 'see' his child. A crisis is set in motion when Baxter's father puzzles over his strange lapses of memory—he forgets the colour of his wife's eyes, then his housekeeper's and finally his son's. This temporary amnesia is like the terminal stage in some deeper loss of being, an inner darkness has begun to invade the very mechanism of sight. If memory is an expression of the soul, then this father has few entries in the records of his emotional history. Every detail in the story reflects this underlying diminution of being—an 'absence' that is only intensified by the occasional physical presence in the home. The tenantless cocoon of newspaper and tobacco smoke can only manage to answer questions 'vaguely', 'absentmindedly' or 'as if quoting himself'. Yet ironically, like some dim memory, the imprisoned spirit stirs treacherously within the carefully fabricated persona of the business man. But since he is not 'at home' in language, either, he can only adopt a worn set of clichés to defuse anxiety. The intuition that there is something wrong is plastered over with complacent platitudes for he never wrestles with the problem of discovering an idiom that will give authentic utterance to his deepest feelings. Language, like a child, is one of the gifts of life, yet this man is unable to internalise the meaning of either. He glosses over his wife's departure with the phrase 'she had run off' and never gets beyond this trite formula other than to muse that 'his marriage to her had been so brief that it were almost as though Baxter were a gift somebody had awarded him, and that as the gift increased in value and liability, his own relation to it was more and more ambiguous and obscure'. Thus 'Baxter' is merely a word and its impingement upon his own self is deflected with commonplace statements as to the mysteriousness of all children or the impossibility of ever knowing another human being.

Our attention is drawn to the defensive nature of his speech, its awkward inflexions and the way in which words are re-arranged to accommodate uneasiness. Accordingly, he conjectures that his housekeeper, Mrs Zilke, must be his 'mother' and 'the boy was an infant "brother" he did not know too well and who asked hard questions'. However, the story is shaped in such a manner that his 'reading' and 're-writing' of relationships is consistently undermined. The toy crocodile that shares Baxter's bed has its own sinister eloquence. It prompts him to agree readily to a suggestion that the boy be given a dog, though here again a gift is to remain an abstraction. When the father evades questions as to whether he had ever had a dog, and even proves incapable of thinking up a *name* for the animal, his son's disappointment is complete. Baxter's announcement that he doesn't want 'anything' has an unwitting accuracy. The sad precociousness of the child's speech is a reflection of his fatherless condition. He realises intuitively that he is being defrauded of the potential gifts of life and that the paid housekeeper and the statutory dog are poor substitutes for the love of a parent.

This knowledge is translated into a curious protest when he conceals in his mouth the wedding ring his father had removed in a gesture implying that its significance had finally evaporated and that even as a label it was now defunct. Baxter's refusal to part with this 'golden toy' draws together the other allusions to the gifts and promises which have never meaningfully been his. It is an unconscious retaliation for his father's inability to invest the outward forms and symbols of human unity with personal connotations. (The word 'son' sounds queer and faintly nauseous when he tries it out.) In the ensuing struggle the ring is forced from his

mouth, but not without Baxter finally giving voice to his depriva-
ation. He shouts out his hatred and kicks his parent squarely in
the groin, prior to making an escape punctuated by an obscene
word. The direct blow to the seat of fatherhood quickly dissipates
the dream-like aura which had obscured the relation to the son and
serves as an appropriate chastisement. The two of them are united
temporarily, if only by a common bond of pain.

Another story in this collection, 'Why Can't They Tell You
Why?', gives a more harrowing account of the chaos brought in
the wake of a father's disappearance. In this instance the parent is
dead, in every sense. We learn from the opening words that 'Paul
knew nothing of his father until he found the box of photographs
on the backstairs'. The magical series of pictures, tracing the
growth from infancy to maturity of the author of his existence,
becomes a treasured possession. He clings onto them as if they
formed the only clue or blueprint to the shadowy life around him.
In every other respect his confusion is so deep that he has been
labelled as mentally ill. His mother, or rather Ethel, as she insists
on being called, is like the parent in 'Color of Darkness' in that
she recoils from the admission of age her child seems to force upon
her. 'I suppose you think I'm a thousand years old,' she snarls,
when he inadvertently calls her 'Mama Ethel'. She would suppress
all evidence of his relation to her and the dead husband is scarcely
mentioned or only referred to mysteriously as 'your father'. Ironically, the only time the boy experiences relief from his world of
darkness is when he hears himself and the photographs discussed
over the telephone in the nightly conversations between Ethel and
one of her friends—a psychologist.

The story centres upon the mother's menacing interrogation of
her child after he has been found on the backstairs, slumped pro-
tectively over his box, in the middle of the night. He has no words
to tell her 'why' he must look at the photographs and she refuses
to interpret the terrible 'language' his actions compose. He is
worried by the command to explain himself like a 'little man' for
the phrase resounds ominously with suggestions of everything that
is beyond his grasp. Ethel's aversion to her son and her inability
to see him as such is conveyed by precise qualifications of her
speech. The frequency and imaginative detail of these form a distinctive feature of the author's style; he seeks to communicate the

total process of which the spoken word is only the surface manifestation. Thus the mother is described as uttering the cruellest
threats to have Paul taken away to a mental asylum with bars,
'in a quiet patient voice like a woman who has endured every
unreasonable disrespectful action from a child who she still can
patiently love'. But there is no 'asylum' for as the one fragile hold
on sanity is severed, the boy's imprisoned spirit is extinguished.

In the flickering light of the basement furnace, Ethel coolly
delivers the impossible ultimatum that he choose between her and
his 'dead' father. The distraught child is before the open door of
hell, his worst nightmare has come true. Yet we are brought to
view him through the distorting lens of the woman's own sickness.
Attention is focused upon the minute modifications of perception
that denote the various stages in her diminishing vision. She
draws back from his entreating touch, from the frenzied petting
of the fur on her slippers and encapsulates each image of distress
as confirmatory evidence of mental illness—the prime cause of
which is now recognised in the obsessive attachment to an old box
of photographs. She imagines she is 'seeing' him for the first time,
'noting with surprise how thin and puny he was, and how dis-
gusting was one small mole that hung from his starved-looking
throat'. Revulsion is succeeded by incredulity as he runs in frantic
circles, clutching the precious box. In her eyes he is nothing more
than a panic-stricken bird or a wounded animal in its death throes.
The final image is horrific: the child crouches in a peculiar position,
hissing savagely, 'while from his mouth black thick strings of
something slipped out, as though he had spewed out the heart of
his grief'. Her nausea is complete.

In such stories Purdy compiles a revised version of the family
album, one in which his parent figures are often portrayed as
having reduced themselves to the lifeless dimensions of photographs. But the images of their arrest in time and in the ignorance
of self-love spring from a different system of optics, they are reproduced in the inner eye of compassion. This chronicle of family
relations is elegiac in tone, it deals in fading pictures, brooding
over the loss of its characters and the failure of love within the
very trinity that customarily denotes human union and inter-
dependency. But although the child-parent bond is a major theme
in both the stories and the novels, the father is distinguished more

by his absences. He is reclassified as a 'missing person' and his disappearance cuts at the very roots of the child's ability to grow towards an understanding of his own identity, leaving him bereft of a guide to the adult world. The absent father symbolises more than the peculiar brand of solipsism exhibited by the business man in 'Color of Darkness'; after all, Paul's father can hardly be accused of abdicating responsibility when he lost his life in the war. Instead, this missing person becomes the focus for an elusive feeling that there is something terribly wrong with life. The child's yearning for an omnipotent being who might transform a painful and bewildering world into something corresponding with its wishes is developed as the metaphor of a more universal condition. This may explain why so many of Purdy's adult characters seem curiously child-like. In fact, the parent in 'Color of Darkness' appears to know far less of the real nature of life than his small son, just as Ethel in 'Why Can't They Tell You Why?' is included in the incomprehension that the title articulates before the mysterious process of growing old and suffering. Such immaturity is also hinted at by the equivocal title of a subsequent work, *Children is All* (1962).

Two of the stories in this later collection show how this missing figure is hopefully invested with god-like powers, capable of assuaging every wound. The first of these, 'Home by Dark', describes a conversation between a child and his grandfather. It gives a beautiful, moving account of the way the child's mind hovers around the fact of his parents' death and of the manœuvres the old man engages in to delay this encounter with grief. The little rituals that make up their day are concluded by the two of them sitting out on the porch, watching the birds in the gathering dusk as they prepare for their migration southwards. But the patterns that confer meaning on their life together are caught up helplessly within the larger movements of time. As with the birds, there seems to be some inner mechanism in the boy which triggers off a restlessness and a curiosity that can scarcely be restrained by the grandfather's tenderness and protective care. He tries to deflect the child's conversation from the South and its associations with the parents' death, speaking with great conviction of the tooth that is to be placed under his pillow that night. He evokes the comforting myths of childhood, elaborating on good fairies and pots of gold. But their talk becomes fraught with unforeseen pit-falls; the South exercises a compulsive hold over the boy's imagina-tion and all his wishes revolve around living with his parents again. He speaks falteringly of the good fairy as being 'somebody dead', or retracts his wish when he reads from his grandfather's face that somehow he has strayed into another area beyond the old man's powers of explanation. 'Well, let's talk about things we can tell each other,' the child concludes, sadly, as if he too would extend an infinite protection.

But in the background of their conversation the night closes in relentlessly, colouring their words and foreshadowing the child's growing sense of oppression. His thoughts trace elliptical patterns, venturing out towards the magnetic South and then turning in desperate flight to regain the safety of his grandfather's presence—to return 'home by dark'. When the tooth in question proves to be missing, the child is inconsolable; the old man's previous insistence on the truth of his folklore now gives the lie to assertions that any night will do for the operation of the wish. The spell is broken and all hope of a magical transformation fades away. There is no supernatural figure, no word or explanation that can postpone the inevitable consciousness of pain. The grandfather can only hold the boy close to him and shut his ears to 'the sounds that came out now like a confused and trackless torrent, making ridiculous the quiet of the evening'.

Although the other story, 'Daddy Wolf', is quite different in tone, it is similarly concerned with the breakdown of hope. In-stead of the pot of gold a mythic parent will exchange for the tooth that is the child's token of growing up, we are given an image of the city's failure to redeem the promises it seems to have ex-tended to those in search of a new and better home. Benny lives on in a rat-infested apartment after his wife and child have aban-doned the attempt to realise that national dream. He is an item of human wreckage and can speak for a long line of failures whose disillusionment is deposited in layers of dirt in the 'linoleum apart-ment' that is falling to pieces around him. Here we have one of the 'missing' fathers, but ironically he has remained child-like in the innocent belief that life will somehow reward his expectations of it. 'Newyorkcity' is invested with all the potency of a seignorial estate where the patrimony and birthright can be claimed. No-one

17

comes to his aid, though, and the whole story deals with Benny's desire to be 're-connected with a certain party' he has been cut off from. The context is ostensibly that of a telephone conversation, but it also images the search for some higher caring authority who will restore a troubled faith.

Overwhelmed by her problems, his wife had made use of a service called the 'Trouble Phone' run by a man known as 'Daddy Wolf'. But despite the coy familiarity with which it advertised itself, the patronage extended only to 'ladies' and the advice dispensed, namely the necessity of church-going and the importance of reading up-lifting books when beset by sexual desires, was grotesquely inadequate, never varying, and sounded suspiciously like a pre-recorded message. In the search for his own 'Daddy Wolf', Benny is obliged to telephone complete strangers in the hope of alleviating his distress.

The form of the story is such that his torrent of words is directed at an unidentified passer-by, perhaps someone waiting to use the phone where Benny anticipates his re-connection to the person picked at random from the directory to be the recipient of his haunting confidences. The reader is placed in an analogous position to these strangers, suddenly 'connected' to an intimate voice which contrasts starkly to the desperate means it has had recourse to. There is both comedy and pathos in his speech as the homely, small town idioms struggle to give shape to the anonymous, ghostly feel of city life: 'I don't object to animals, see. If it had been a Mama bird, say, which had come out of the hole, I would have had a start, too, as a Mama bird seldom is about and around at that hour, not to mention it not nesting in a linoleum hole, but I think I feel the way I do just because you think of rats along with neglect and lonesomeness and not having nobody near or around you.' Such complete lack of sophistication or duplicity endears him to the reader, but it renders him ill-equipped to survive a world spawned between 'Daddy Wolf' and 'Mama rat'. The only semblance of paternal care the city affords is the 'Trouble Phone', but like those who seek its aid, it cannot accommodate reality. Though Benny's anguish had been calmed by that certain party's willingness to act as audience to his grief, we learn that polite interjections of 'I see' had been the only response to his 'emergency phone call' before it was brought to an abrupt close.

18

Our willingness to listen places us uneasily in the same dilemma; it is hard to escape our 'connection' when Benny blurts out comments such as: 'I raise the lever that sews the lining to *your* mittens.'

The image of the orphaned or deserted child is given its most sombre treatment in the novella *63: Dream Palace*, which is included in the collection *Color of Darkness*. It lends a particular force to this overall title by its reconstruction of the shadowy underworld beneath the brightly-lit surface of city life. The small child's nightmare in 'Why Can't They Tell You Why?', described as 'the complete and final fear of what may happen in living', is reproduced on a larger scale. The novella depicts each sinister step in the tragic process of destruction that engulfs two youths in their parentless world. At one point, Fenton Riddleway stands forlornly outside a wrestling arena known as 'Fair City', 'as though asking somebody for an admission ticket'. This suggests in microcosm his exclusion from the Promised Land the city has come to symbolise in his desperate need and the story as a whole assesses the price to be paid for entry into this mythical realm.

After the death of their mother, Fenton and his younger brother, Claire, leave their small town home in West Virginia. They are drawn to the city in the hope that a friend, Kincaid, will help them find work. However, the designated meeting place turns out to be a rotting house in a derelict area of 63rd Street. Like Benny, they wait on in misery to be 're-connected'. But the mysterious Kincaid, as if he were the very spirit of this world, never lives up to the promise of his name. His rejection of a paternal role is to become a familiar pattern.

We are introduced to Fenton through the recollections of an aspiring writer, Parkhearst Cratty, and an eccentric wealthy widow, Grainger, described rather ominously as the 'Queen of Hell' by the former. It is appropriate that he should exist for them only as a story and as the memory of a mysterious being, for both failed to respond to the youth's needs, preferring to see him as a novel accessory to the peculiar performances they have substituted for spontaneous behaviour. In consequence, his self remains as enigmatic as his actual name, even though he made an indelible impression on their lives and left them fascinated by what he 'did'. Despite the fact that 'real' things were never mentioned at

Grainger's, they feel compelled to review all their knowledge of him, as if obliquely recognising this failure to accommodate reality.

Fenton's story seems to hold the key to their dissatisfaction with life; they seek an answer to the recurrent feeling of enduring a living death. Yet this world weariness is more properly the key to our understanding of the youth's destruction and their conversation forms a highly significant preamble to the ensuing narrative. In particular, Parkhearst laments that he was always unable to capture his subject on paper because he could never discover who he was. Since this ignorance of identity applies equally well to himself, it is appropriate that Parkhearst's voice should fade into the darkness that he and Grainger essentially inhabit as Purdy takes over the narrative of Fenton's disintegration. Parkhearst's failure becomes the 'eyepiece' of his own account. The would-be writer represents the tendency to turn life into a fiction-making process which is depicted as a general phenomenon in this world. It is only poetic justice that he should in turn be reduced to the status of a character in somebody else's story, particularly one which addresses itself to his habitual question: 'Why are we dead anyhow?' Whereas Fenton is a stranger to Parkhearst's vocabulary, the youth's own words have conferred a lingering reality on the world of Grainger and her disciple. For example, the house where they rehearse their undecipherable memories is customarily referred to as the 'mansion' ever since he breathed life into it by giving it that name.

The aspiring writer comes to be seen as a familiar figure in Purdy's work. In addition to the symbolic function already mentioned, the author seems attracted to the device precisely because it has become something of a commonplace—worn-out forms in literature and everyday language are favourite targets for his irony. It is as if he tackled all manifestations of arrested life, 're-cycling' clichéd patterns to forge a more meaningful and personalised idiom. The final effect is to disclose a mysterious infrastructure at the heart of the familiar world.

In this instance, the 'writer' roams one of the central parks looking for and treating people like 'material'. His fellow wanderers are likened to 'shades in hell' and their aimless drifting in an atmosphere of death sets the tone for the whole city. If Grainger is the 'Queen of Hell', then Parkhearst, as his name suggests, is one of her wardens, a purveyor of stories and specimens to supply novelty to his monarch's jaded appetite. (It is no accident, either, that both appear to have lost their 'christian' name.) At a moment when Parkhearst is fretting over the uneventful nature of existence and feeling that he deserves a reward for mere endurance, he comes across Fenton. His immediate association of the youth with the word 'reward' signifies his habit of pre-defining experience. For a while he feigns indifference, secretly translating the apparition into a symbol of wildness and freedom. But as he listens to the pleas for help, he is soon worried at the prospect of involvement in something more than a story. During this assessment of his 'material' potential, the youth has an uncanny understanding of the failure of responsibility that is taking place. He quickly decides that 'this was only a listener who having heard the story would let him go back to the "not right house" '.

There are many ironies in this encounter of 'writer' and 'material'. In a deeper sense, Fenton *is* the very material of life —of its pain, of the need for love, and of the misery of growing up in a 'not right' world without a guide or interpreter. Purdy's 'performance' brings Parkhearst face to face with the element he excludes from his own. Ironically, the author dresses Fenton for his part in a manner which even Parkhearst recognises as peculiarly significant. He feels 'there was something about this boy too excessive; everything about him was too large for him, the speech, the terrible clothes, the ragged hair, the possible gun, the outlandish accent'. Yet he wilfully ignores his true meaning by refusing to decipher the language of utter desperation. When he does finally visit the boy, the only form of assistance offered is an introduction to Grainger and so he relinquishes the dangerous sensations of being in contact with 'real' suffering. Fenton, who had been searching for a 'way out', is given a set of directions that leads into the labyrinth of self destruction the writer already inhabits. The latter inverts the role of father, just as Grainger is a travesty of a mother. Neither have come to terms with adulthood; like perverse children they construct a fantasy world to shut out the pain of being alive. The introduction to the 'great woman' will bring about the 'birth' of Fenton's new self. Time flows backwards.

Grainger, with her cavernous, mascara-rimmed eyes, presides over this dark world like some malevolent Mother Goddess. The complete discrepancy between her outward behaviour and inner thoughts is brought out most clearly with regard to her former husband, Russell. She pretended to have loved him passionately whilst claiming he never really cared for her at all. However, Parkhearst, familiar with her brand of self-deception, is able to inform us that in fact Russell had loved her madly whereas she simply acted a part which his sudden death obliged her to perpetuate. Grainger has even erected a memorial to her late husband, consisting of a room full of photographs, old clothes and flowers, privately likened to a 'church' by Parkhearst. The memorial is apt, for we are told that Russell, an ironic variant on the 'missing' father, was little more than a blank Grainger dressed up in the costumes of her fantasies. By her refusal to commit herself to the actual suffering of love, Grainger's 'church' is more of a monument to the death of her feeling self. Her life is reduced to a series of hollow gestures, a curious medley of theatrical performances. Accordingly, Russell's death is preceded by a burlesque version of *Romeo and Juliet* whilst on another occasion Parkhearst observes that she is managing to look 'a little too much like Hamlet's mother'.

Fenton is to be captured and incorporated into the 'great woman's' performance; she announces drunkenly that he *is* Russell and goes on to present him with the clothes of that 'dead young Christ'. He has been offered a leading role, with stupendous costumes, in the dream world that characterises the city and its inhabitants. Yet what is enacted is a blasphemous version of the family unit which corresponds to Fenton's notion that the whole world has begun to move backwards for him. This anticipates the terrible ambiguity of his last words to Claire; Parkhearst doesn't help him forward into manhood, but leads him back down to an infernal region where he becomes—a 'motherfucker'.

In complete antithesis to Grainger's 'dream palace' is the derelict building on 63rd Street which houses the despair of Fenton and his young brother. Their relationship is juxtaposed with the anonymous underworld of the park, the All-Night Theatre, and Grainger's entertainments. Its destruction is registered as the necessary price for admission to this circle of shadows. The murder of Claire, and with him Fenton's own deepest self, is long foreseen as an inevitable sacrifice. Fenton himself feels the city's

22

darkness closing in on them and is haunted by the notion that it is 'late' out, the 'latest' time in his life and perhaps the 'latest' in the whole world. His sense of an impending doom springs from within the house too; since there seems to be no way of ensuring their future together, Claire's urgent need of him is torture. On occasion the frustrations of an impotent love lead him to strike the boy. At other times he seeks relief in haunts such as the All-Night Theatre where 'somebody's hand sometimes came out of the dark and touched you as though to determine whether you were flesh or not'. But though this seems to offer a release from the problems and pains of selfhood, the dead shadows that flicker on the screen simply mirror the unreality of the audience and the city beyond.

Fenton cannot reconcile Claire's and his mother's belief in a loving God with the derelict, bug-ridden world he finds himself in. God is the ultimate 'missing' father and thus the image of the orphan acquires a wider, religious meaning. The youth reacts with a sort of furious despair as the myth collides helplessly with his actual experience of the city. It is significant that whereas Fenton tries to understand his inner turmoil by writing things down in his 'notepapers', Parkhearst manipulates language as something abstract and apart from himself, enjoying the mere sound of his own voice. The latter's dislocation of the inner life from outward forms of expression is to be Fenton's ultimate destination; on one level he journeys into a 'foreign' language. These divisions are shaped in the relationship between the two brothers. As Fenton explores the city in search of a way *out*, Claire spends more and more time *in* the room, populating it with his fears and desires, listening to the sounds in his own psyche. In common with the children in previous stories, Claire symbolises that bewildered hope for love, a part of him his brother must forsake or destroy if he is to adopt the only role the 'adult' world has offered him. Claire is the ideal self which refuses to compromise with the sordid commerce of life. Each brother pursues his separate dream until their essential unity is severed. The two houses correspond to these extremes in an ironic fashion: Grainger's 'dream palace' conceals an inner vacuum, whereas the house on 63rd Street gives a precarious home to the values of love and caring despite its façade of dereliction and rottenness. There seems to be no hope of reconcil-

23

ing the two. Claire's fervent religious feelings have their only counterpart in Grainger's memorial to her non-existent love, the 'church' dedicated to the 'dead young Christ'. This is not the 'real' house Claire yearns for.

The final onslaught comes, appropriately enough, in the guise of a visit to the theatre. Fenton leaves Claire after a quarrel over his refusal to take up residence with him at Grainger's. He is picked up by Parkhearst's replica, a young man called Bruno Korsawski, and taken to a performance of *Othello*. The play itself is a mere pretext for one of Bruno's actor friends, Hayden Banks, to show off his talents. Hayden, and not the author, is hailed as the 'genius of the spoken word'! Fenton, on the other hand, is suspicious of words and distinguishes himself by uttering very few during the interminable introductions to Bruno's friends. In fact, he dozes off as the play is performed, although he does manage to break wind conspicuously in the middle of the loftier flights of rhetoric. His lapses, both from decorum and from consciousness, suggest an ironic comment on the corruption of language in this world and its relegation to use as an instrument of deception. All the people he meets are assemblages of verbal disguises and expect him to be the same. For example, Bruno exclaims over the name 'Fenton Riddleway'—'That's the most interesting name I have ever heard. Is it your own?' At another level, though, the question is highly pertinent. Fenton's identity is rapidly receding and the name he has inherited seems to connect him with no-one. It pinpoints the underlying metaphysical preoccupations of the story—just who is his ultimate 'maker' or 'author'?

It is unfortunate that Fenton is not more selective in his suspicions of language for the substance of the play has an urgent bearing upon his situation. It is significant that Othello's tragedy stems from the destructive power of false words and culminates in the murder of the person he most cherished, in a travesty of his former self. Although the play is grossly overacted, there is, for once, evidence of words serving a deeply human purpose. Fenton's indiscriminate antipathy renders him the more vulnerable; afterwards we learn of 'the young man who played Iago and who looked even more like a valentine devil off stage whispering in his ear'. The confusion of illusion and reality which infects his grasp of his true allegiances reaches its climax at the subsequent party in

Hayden Banks' flat. The huge murals of the ocean mirror his stance at the brink of Hades, the actor's domain. The motif of entry into a dream world suggested by the formlessness of water is continued in the youth's determined consumption of both alcohol and marijuana. In angry haste to master the rituals of this society he snatches at drugged cigarettes and fills himself with drink. His experiences of the city converge; each interior reproduces another, the people and their drugs are the same and the youth is lost in a deadly haze. However, some last vestige of integrity causes him to rebel against the process of dissolution. When Bruno undresses him mechanically, he hits out. Yet the full force of this violence is felt elsewhere as he disappears into the night to murder Claire, playing the part of the 'stranger' he had tried to frighten his brother with earlier.

In the light of the morning, the young boy is discovered in the filthy, bug-ridden cot with his neck broken. For a while Fenton wonders joyfully over the 'reality' of Claire in comparison to the people around them and goes through the motions of talking to the body and feeding it with rolls and coffee. But the dream soon breaks and the obsession with the 'lateness' of everything releases its potent irony. In this sombre view of the world a symbolic burial forms the final rite of initiation and we are left with an image of the 'service' or 'funeral' Fenton forces himself to carry out. He remembers a wooden chest in the attic where there are a few cobwebbed pictures on the wall, one of Jesus amongst the thieves, another of a poem concerning Mother Love. In a savage contrast to the 'church' where Grainger had decorated over a blank, a real body is committed to its final resting place. The dream of love is relegated to memory; it is now little more than a broken relic in mankind's attic. The last picture is of Fenton kissing the dead stained lips before struggling with the stinking corpse upstairs to the chest where a torn wedding veil will serve as shroud. He utters the words: 'Up we go then, motherfucker.'

The profanity is a telling epitaph upon the two brothers. In an immediate sense it sums up the youth's disappearance within a 'foreign' language, his grief being clamped down under a mask. But at the same time the word is rooted in an agonised sense of the violation of the natural order of things that has taken place. It encompasses *both* their destinies: Claire is simultaneously that part of Fenton which is sacrificed and returned to the dream of Mother Love, and an image of the 'being' the city has now reduced him to. There is nothing to add to his biography if the word is used to denote the history of a 'living' person. Thus we are told that the fissure opened up by his brother's death 'marked the limits of a line, not ending his youth but making his youth superfluous, as age to a god'.

In Purdy's first novel, *Malcolm* (1959), the dialectic of innocence and experience is again dramatised in terms of an orphaned youth seeking his way in a world from which his father has mysteriously disappeared. This time the author's comic genius is in full evidence, although events are still charged with an underlying sadness which gives the surface humour a particularly incisive quality.

In some ways it would seem that the materials and themes of *63: Dream Palace* were being viewed through the other end of a telescope. Whereas Fenton's predicament was terribly real and immediate, Malcolm's adventures are rendered in comic form by means of a distancing effect. But the author's technical strategies are highly conscious arbiters of meaning and this detachment forms a deliberate parody of the compulsion to fictionalise reality which all his characters are possessed by. One of them, Madame Girard, utters the dictum that 'Texture is all . . . substance nothing' and Purdy creates a novelistic form to act as an ironic mirror to this process of loss. The approach bears an interesting relation to the proposition that the finished work of art is somehow diminished and entrapped when it is given public form (an idea that preoccupies George Steiner in his book *Language and Silence*) for Purdy emphatically simulates such an impression in *Malcolm* whilst turning it to his own advantage. In his mind it is not so much the finished work of art but life itself that has been the subject of this reductive process. Consequently, a stasis of form functions as the metaphor of a state of arrest which has infected all human relationships.

On the surface, *Malcolm*, is made up of a picaresque sequence of adventures which have all the ingenuous charm of a fairy tale. In the tradition of folklore an infant of royal descent is lost to his true parents, but in this version something goes wrong and the revelation of identity never takes place. Our expectations of a parable of the innocent's initiation into the adult world are ironically undermined. Within the contours of a familiar story there is a constant feeling of an elusive meaning that has somehow severed itself from events and people. It is as if the characters retain a dim memory of what this traditional life-story ought to be like, but in practice its essence always escapes them. The novel's 'texture' mimics this sense of loss with much humour and ingenuity. Its manner recalls the description of Marlow, in Joseph Conrad's *Heart of Darkness*, for whom 'the meaning of an episode was not inside like a kernel but outside, enveloping the tale which brought it out only as a glow brings out a haze, in the likeness of one of these misty halos that sometimes are made visible by the spectral illumination of moonshine'.

Malcolm seems to embody this essence of life and his problematic involvements with other people demonstrate the degree to which that ideal recedes from their touch. His origins are obscure, or only dimly suggested by the whispering sea-shells he loves to listen to in the privacy of his hotel suite. He appears to have no surname and might almost be the product of some Immaculate Conception, for, in this instance, the absent father is imbued with celestial associations. The latter's disappearance or possible death has brought an abrupt end to the idyllic togetherness when father and son travelled from one palatial hotel to another in the course of their 'business'. Motion is replaced by immobility and the opening image is of the youth sitting patiently on an ornamental, golden bench. All the allusions to Malcolm's past hint at his present exclusion from some edenic realm pre-dating consciousness and it is no accident that he gives the impression of being a foreigner, even to the language. His eager confession that he is little more than a blank or cypher is as ambiguous as the whiteness of Melville's whale. In one sense it is the consequence of his severance from his father and some heavenly realm of perfect love, and in another sense it denotes his purity and innocence of the ways of the world. It suggests both the absence and the plenitude of meaning. But instead of a 'marriage' between Malcolm and the world that incites him to motion, he seems even blanker (if that is possible) by the end of the novel. In retrospect, then, there is much irony in Mr Cox's indignant pronouncement that the boy seemed *'wedded'* (author's italics) to his bench.

27

The disappearance of Malcolm's father is unexplained and as the novel proceeds his very existence is thrown into question. One suspects his empire is in ruins since there is little 'holy' business to transact in a civilisation Mr Cox likes to think of as his personal responsibility. With a sardonic pun, the author suggests that 'Cox' have altogether usurped the larger meanings of paternity. Little wonder the youth's aura of divine love produces an uneasiness in the Professor. The sight of him waiting endlessly on an ornamental bench delivers an obscure threat to his whole philosophy; he can see no 'earthly or practical purpose' in such a stance. If Malcolm's total inertia offers a criticism of his own existence, it is because he calls into question the whole point of movement in a world where the bonds of love have been broken. Mr Cox is his exact opposite; as the most famous astrologer of his 'depleted epoch' and its greatest walker, he has great confidence in the plotting and execution of different kinds of movement. If Malcolm is the picture of inward contemplation, Mr Cox always looks outside of himself to discover purposes and signs in life. But although the latter devotes himself to the study of the heavens and pretends to chart their influence on terrestial affairs, ironically he cannot recognise the offspring of some celestial body in a face to face encounter. Despite the boy's pronounced air of expectancy and his waiting for a 'father', the astrologer vehemently rejects any possibility of his being called upon to make restitution of such a claim. The boy's plea to be taken home with him is ruled 'out of the question'. He will not pursue the meaning of his orphaned status, 'for the subjects of tragedy and death were most unwelcome to him'.

Mr Cox has arrogantly substituted patterns of chance for the natural bonds of mutual responsibility. A tyrannous figure, he has mushroomed into the void of a godless world like some magician or satanic guru. He thrives on the exercise of power over people as if this were the only remaining absolute in an otherwise vacant world. The possession of this 'truth' allows him to function as a confidence man, malevolently instilling directions into the lives of his puppets since they have long lost any inner sense of guidance. Thus Malcolm is ordered to give himself up to 'things'. The word is suitably vague (or 'firmly evasive' to borrow Madame Girard's description of her mentor), for the realm he directs him

28

to is lacking in human and even in solid material dimensions. Accordingly, the youth is provided with 'addresses' rather than friendship, prised off his bench to be made to conform to the laws of motion and so to 'begin'.

Unfortunately, Mr Cox's plans for Malcolm never quite *materialise* and this failure leads him to reflect briefly on others. He complains that though he had brought the right people into the right situations, somehow they failed to 'act' and nothing happened. The Professor is the precursor of many artist figures in the novel and it soon becomes clear that Malcolm has his own introductions to bestow, in the sense that he brings them face to face with the spiritual possibilities they exclude from creation. Although the astrologer determines to be the author of his existence, the boy is never 'at home' in any of the settings provided. He unwittingly shows up the 'blankness' of each scenario and, indeed, the 'BLANC EMPIRE MORTUARY' forms his first and only port of call.

Thus the youth's visit to the undertaker, Estel Blanc, is simultaneously an initiation ceremony and a performance of the last rites. In a doom-laden atmosphere of incense, the mortician (prematurely retired since he has lost the inspiration of his art!) makes perfunctory conversation which eventually has the same choking effect on Malcolm as the sickly Spanish chocolate he is plied with. Later, they are regaled with a peculiar solo number by a certain Cora Naldi, a remnant of the funeral choir. She is a siren-like harbinger of dissolution, of movements that escape meaning or definition. We are told that 'Malcolm was never able to tell anybody later what or who Cora Naldi was. He was not even sure at times she was a woman, for she had a very deep voice, and he could never tell whether her hair was white, or merely platinum, or whether she was coloured like Estel or white like himself.' The youth's reaction to this plethora of contradictory data is to lapse from consciousness, a response which is to become characteristic of him and a humorously apt evaluation of his experiences. He cannot even grasp the reasons for his host's displeasure, for, like Fenton before him, he is adrift in a 'foreign' language where words rarely seek to engage with the reality of another person. Whilst rehearsing the possible reasons for Malcolm's apparent prejudice against him, the mortician points out largely for his own benefit that 'undertaking is perhaps the most aesthetic of all professions and indeed the most universal'. The comment has a sardonic reference beyond its immediate context in its intimations of art's subservience to death. It images Purdy's horror at the 'embalment' which has resulted from the usurpation of creative skills. Life has been invaded by a false kind of artistry, it has become a construction of texture without substance. The black undertaker's name is another sign of this negation; he is a star without light, a purveyor of darkness. Such contradictions of word and meaning have their counterpart in the overall shape of the narrative. Its linear movement proves deceptive for the episode with Estel Blanc has given a preview of the concluding funeral ceremony, one which is brought on by Malcolm's introduction to another 'star'.

Since he proves insufficiently 'ripe' to benefit from Estel Blanc's artistry, Malcolm is passed on to Address No. 2, where he meets Kermit and Laureen Raphaelson. According to Professor Cox, everybody who counts is married and therefore it is a subject Malcolm must begin to consider in relation to himself. However, he soon concludes from this introduction to the desirable state that married love is the strangest 'thing' of all. The Raphaelsons enact an outrageous parody of marital relations, each treating the other as their private 'doll' and conducting fierce battles and deceitful campaigns of affection. The youth is the bewildered spectator of a manic Punch and Judy show and, like the unfortunate baby in that tradition, he is alternately squabbled over or ignored. Even when the flow of language is directed at him, his host is quite unperturbed by his confession that he will probably not listen at all since it is too overpowering. Malcolm is particularly mystified by the couple's disproportionate sizes: Laureen is large, plump and commanding, whereas Kermit is a tiny child-like creature who will admit to being neither a midget nor a dwarf. The image of arrested development sums up their relationship. Laureen is like a mother indulging in an erotic fantasy life centering upon her 'little man', at least until a Japanese wrestler whisks her off to sample the 'real equipment'. Kermit is merely her plaything, like the cats which she alternately petted or was cruel to as if they were extensions of his personality. The attempt to reduce life to a desired shape is epitomised by the artistry Kermit employs in carving beautiful chairs to fit his tiny frame. This constant shaping and abstracting has its verbal equivalent in the frequent commands they issue in a last ditch attempt to order their world by the assertion of sheer strength.

If the Raphaelsons' love-making resembles a Punch and Judy show, Malcolm's subsequent visit to the Girards propels him into a soap opera on a magnificent scale. In fact he is greeted by one of their acolytes with the information that he is just in time for the evening performance. Madame Girard amplifies the previous couple's dissatisfactions with marriage in an imperious manner, bewailing her suffering at the hands of her husband in regal histrionics before a spell-bound audience of identical young men. It is significant that she should initially denounce Malcolm as a spy of Mr Cox, for her poorly dissimulated fear of that gentleman (and the concept of sexuality he represents) points to her life-long battle to preserve an illusion of independent self-creation. Like Laureen, she identifies happiness with the era before Mr Cox became her mentor. We are told, at a later point, when she reviews Girard's courtship of her, that as his ring was thrust on her finger, changes appeared all around her like the cracks in an ice floe. The imagery is apt, for in resisting the sexual and sacrificial connotations in the placing of the ring, she freezes the possibilities of selfhood. Instead of immersing in the moving current of life, whatever its pain and suffering, Madame Girard can only win a hollow victory by cutting herself off from the deepest rhythms of her body and indulging in a ceremonious worship of youth. Her loves are of the 'candle-lighting type' and as long as her husband is content to worship her as an ideal and seek sexual satisfaction with his laundresses, there is 'order' in her empire. Or a semblance of such, until Malcolm appears like the very spectre of vanished youth and she must make him her own. His princely charm is even greater since, like Kermit, he is only a 'little man' and cannot threaten her supremacy.

Madame Girard is a wonderfully comic creation, but there are moments when she is also deeply involved in the novel's underlying pathos. One such occasion is when Girard Girard leaves her to seek the 'real equipment' in Laureen Raphaelson. Her reign seems over, primarily because she cannot contemplate life without her name. The chapter has the ironic heading 'Leave me Madame Girard' and deals with her terror at the idea of being stripped of

31

her title. The substantial monetary and psychological comforts the marriage had blessed her with are of minor importance in comparison. Her husband argues: 'Your young friends, your young men, will come to see what is you. Your pure victory, as you have always called it, is now. You are completely free—can't you see?' But we understand the sad logic of her abject pleading to be left 'Madame Girard' for her whole existence has dwindled to a mere name and her identity has no inner dimensions to sustain its loss.

Purdy develops an informing thematic pattern from the way names are experienced by different characters. There are many minor instances of the severance of a name from the person it is theoretically attached to, refusals to accept names or attempts to impose names upon other people. For example, when Mr Girard comes to deliver his invitation for Malcolm to spend the summer at his country house, it seems as though he might be acting in a fatherly fashion, extending the patronage of his own illustrious name to the boy who so obviously lacks one. But the gesture is negated when it transpires that he is simply carrying out orders from his wife. When the youth expresses his worry at the idea of leaving the only friends he has in the world, his would-be benefactor exclaims that he doesn't recognise these people 'except by name'. Furthermore, when Malcolm is favoured with the special privilege of calling him by his first name, he is perplexed to discover this is Girard too. Instead of distinguishing the uniqueness of individuals, names seem interchangeable with the empty seashells the youth would put to his ear to capture some whisper of sound. By extension, the language uttered by such characters adds up to 'nothing', as Malcolm reveals when called upon for an account of the extraordinary visit paid him by Girard Girard. He decides that 'if Girard's coming had not been exactly a dream, it had not added up to anything more than his arrival and departure'. For all the 'addresses' Malcolm is subjected to, he is never able to do more than echo wonderingly the waves of sound that break over him.

The episode where the Girards call upon Kermit dramatises the failures of language with many subtle effects, both comic and poignant. It seems that if Kermit could be persuaded to accompany Malcolm to the Girard's country mansion, then life for all of them might begin. However, Kermit is intimidated by his royal visitors and retreats further and further into the dark closet in the depths of his studio as if they were giants from another civilisation. He cannot believe in them and the future they hold out. It is as if Kermit acted out Malcolm's inner feelings, for neither of them is wanted in his own right and the Girards merely project upon them the values they feel to have escaped them in their own existence. Kermit is reduced to speechlessness by their imperious commands, his own reality annihilated by the insuperable barriers their words create. This blockage of communication is translated into vivid images by the doors and panes of glass which cut him off from their dazzling splendour. He is nothing but an 'outline' or 'silhouette' in their eyes, though from Kermit's own point of view they are similarly obscured. Mr Girard, with a rare glimpse of something outside himself, declares that perhaps the 'midget' could have been persuaded to come with them if only they knew what he thought he was. But the effort of giving expression to another person's subjectivity is too much for them and it is left to Madame Girard to quash this potential heresy with the visor-like maxim—'Silhouettes tell all'. There is a comic consistency in her edicts. For example, when she is brought in view of the Japanese-style temples that are associated with her past, she literally pulls down a veil over her eyes as if to ward off any threat to her equanimity. The comment which prescribes her husband's account of his abortive telephone call to Kermit is equally revealing. He is placed under the injunction to tell only what happened and warned: 'If comments or adjectives are to be supplied, we shall do so.' In such a manner, words are reclassified as the instruments of a ruthless ego. There is no authentic interaction between people, only rival attempts to wrest control of the flow of language, in the hope of directing whatever 'story' they feel they are starring in and wish to exercise omniscience over. This stylisation of reality may give an illusion of autonomy but ultimately it defeats its own objective since it brings about the imprisonment of the inner self.

Malcolm's reception at Address No. 4 has all the familiarity of an inevitable ritual. As usual, he is plied with drink, much talked at, but rarely listened to. One of his hosts, Jerome, particularly disconcerts the boy by enveloping him in circuitous conversation and at the same time reaching out to give him odd caresses. His cumulative ambiguities prove too much for Malcolm to cope with and he topples unconscious from his chair. It is worth examining this part of their conversation in detail for it typifies the ironic sense in which speech evaporates in its own vacuity. They are at a point where Jerome has declared that since they both believe in the same thing (though this is unspecified) Malcolm must give up his allegiance to Cox and Girard and devote himself to the wisdom of his present mentor. The boy is stirred into motion by this hint of affinity between them; the word 'belief' (which is reiterated throughout the novel) is connected with the dubious existence of his father and it seems for a moment that he is about to pick up his trail. But the promise of knowledge peters out as Malcolm is *ordered* to sit *still* . . .

'What do we believe in, Malcolm? What a pleasant, pleasant question! I'm so awfully glad you said *we*. I will appreciate that a long time. A hell of a long time from now I will think of that question of yours, Malcolm; what do WE believe in. You carry me right back to something, Malc . . .'

'You see I don't know what I be——'

'Don't spoil it, Malc. Don't say another word.'

'Jerome,' Malcolm's voice came shaky and tiny now.

'Don't spoil anything now' Jerome commanded again, his eyes soft and half-closed. 'Don't speak.'

Like Mr Cox, Jerome is 'firmly evasive' in his beliefs and his words cancel one another out in a manner that is both comic and terrifying. It is no wonder Malcolm feels time has stopped altogether in this household. The atmosphere of a perpetual autumn has invaded even its material substance; it seems to disintegrate visibly, 'owing to some damage perhaps to the machinery of the cosmos'.

Yet on the surface, the pace of the novel seems to be accelerating. Malcolm has left the security of his bench to take up residence in a household full of activity. There are endless jazz concerts in progress on the upper floors, a study of delinquent minors is taking shape in the basement, and Eloisa busies herself with painting somewhere in between. Furthermore, in Mr Cox's terminology, Malcolm has definitely 'begun'—the unconventional sleeping arrangements necessitated by a house full of itinerant musicians provide strange combinations of bedfellows. But underneath all these energies is an ever increasing sense of loss. The youth feels more and more alone, despite the quickening fight for his possession. He had described the Girards as too 'imposing' (borrowing a word), but he is presently subjected to more insidious forms of imposition. When Kermit bluntly asks if he is still a virgin, the reply he elicits is 'not exactly'—Malcolm cannot even be sure if he has passed the demarcation between childhood and adult love. In this twilight world all relationships are deprived of contours and contact, even that of sexuality, surpasses definition. He finds himself neither in a home with people who will provide the affection and guidance of surrogate parents, nor in an environment where he can deduce the principles of growth from the models of behaviour around him.

Paradoxically, many of the conversations he overhears, or is a party to, touch upon the very subjects of love and marriage. But they take place on a level which renders them about as intelligible as a foreign language. Everyone seems to be acting out a role which, in the course of time, has hardened into an impenetrable mask. Each person has made a profession out of the maintenance of a self-image. Jerome has translated his prison years into a book, a sort of manual which issues blueprints for his current relations with people; Eloisa can never manage to paint anything but idealized self-portraits; Madame Girard obliges herself to perform a 'slow distant imitation of love' towards her husband, and so on. The word has come to precede experience, indeed it has all but replaced it completely. As each attempts to project this chosen image, tremendous verbal battles take place whenever its stasis is threatened, with resorts to physical violence if all else fails. It is Madame Girard who exposes much of this sophistry, and incidentally her own, by the sheer scale of her manœuvres to combat the terms that are applied to her. When the present eludes her grasp, she turns her attention to the future. Jerome is withered under the following oracular address,

'I issue a prognostication on you: your "cure" is over! Do you hear? You are no longer "cured". A long set-back is about to overtake you, and you are to go back and learn the lesson you have forgotten from your burglar days, that love is deeds and not honeyed talk.'

Her verbal belligerence culminates in the splendid sermon-like oration she delivers in retaliation for her expulsion from Malcolm's presence. Having trumpeted her impending arrival over the telephone and thereby annihilated Eloisa, she bears down on them all like a warship, giving forth broadsides of 'love', spluttering commands and imperatives in a determination to encompass the entire company in her definitions. She styles herself as some regal Mother whose rebellious children must be brought back firmly under her sway since, she claims, they all depend upon her for their very life.

It is interesting to compare her speech with the Sermon 'God' delivers in *Children is All*. The sense in which her communication is all 'texture' and no 'substance' is put into an ironic perspective by this other heavenly broadcast. His only message is that there is no message. Since His audience will not accept the 'hereness' of their situation they are doomed—'because you will go on trying to be other than you are and therefore you succeed always in continuing as you have been'. The fate of Malcolm's portrait spells out a similar message. Just as various characters construct and relate to their own verbal image of the youth, so Eloisa sets herself to capture his likeness in another medium in a manner which sees *her* portrait and not its actual subject as all-important. Furthermore, Madame Girard insists on purchasing it, as she was expected to, but dismisses the fact that it was scarcely begun as of no conceivable interest. It is only the *idea* of its existence that matters, not the substantial reality—elsewhere she is to describe the youth with unconscious accuracy as 'the idea of her life'. Of course, the final irony is when Eloisa is forced to 'eat' her words: Jerome rules that the balance of power in their marriage should not be altered by monetary windfalls and Madame Girard's cheque is ceremoniously, if not acrimoniously, chewed to pieces. Thus the comic logic of events describes a recurring circle. Nothing 'adds up' and Eloisa's empty canvas gives a more exact portrait of Malcolm's visit.

Only Malcolm is distinguished by a willingness to give himself up to the dynamics of growth. Yet it is this same openness to experience that renders him so attractive to others. Not only is his extreme youth a quality they seek to appropriate, but he can also be tailored to fit the exact shape of their fantasies since he has no fixed identity. However, as soon as he seeks to understand these roles, his would-be possessors ignore his questions or rule them out of order. It is as if any assertion of independence on his part reduces his mirror-function, just as any mention of his father forms an irritating reminder of some limits on the abstractions they wish to superimpose. This explains why the very existence of his father is so frequently questioned, altogether denied or blasphemed —inevitably so, when we consider what that person has come to represent. Such behaviour is exemplified by Girard Girard when he summons the boy peremptorily to an interview in the Horticultural Gardens. After the 'great man' has tried to persuade Malcolm to *choose* him for his *own*, he counters requests for further information with vagueness. The only concrete statement he offers is that the boy has no alternative anyway, since he is now off the bench and has no money to continue at his hotel. The word 'own' is suitably ambiguous, for whilst Girard Girard asks Malcolm to choose him for his own sake, the plea carries no reciprocal acknowledgement of what the boy's own self might be. His real wish is to exercise *ownership*. Like his wife, he only appears to be attracted by things which are beyond his reach. As soon as Malcolm capitulates to his scheme then he is abandoned as summarily as he was called. The youth is a mere pawn in another marital battle; the magnate has a pre-ordained schedule which cannot be modified, least of all by the acquisition of an adoptive son. Thus the exclusion from the palatial hotel is repeated—the boy is shut out of the edenic gardens to wait forlornly in front of the locked gates.

From this point Malcolm's decline is rapid. When events cause him to stray from the circuit of addresses, he is snapped up and offered membership of another exclusive circle. A black motorcyclist whisks him off to meet Melba, a singing star, who proves to be very much a sign of the times. She surrounds herself with 'contemporaries', a privileged coterie of adoring fans with its own stylised vocabulary. Once more Malcolm is engulfed by a 'foreign' language. Melba has stamped her words on a vast public, a process which she continues off-stage when Malcolm is found to coincide exactly with her recipe for a 'contemporary'. This time he allows himself to be taken over completely—'Down payment, lock, stock and barrel', as Melba is later to reflect . . .

Malcolm was about to ask them what a contemporary was, but suddenly his old desire to ask questions deserted him. He found that he

37

did not care now what anything was. Too much had happened, too many people had come and gone in his life, and feeling a sudden warmth and pressure from Melba's hand, he *mechanically* brought this hand to his lips and kissed it.

'I have had such a short long life,' Malcolm said, meaning this remark to be silent and for himself, but by accident the words came out loud and strong, and Melba, extremely pleased by what he had said immediately drank a toast to him. (My italics)

Malcolm no longer seeks to make sense out of the language or the people he encounters. But the involuntary words and strange cooing sounds that escape him compose a vocabulary of 'non-communication' that ironically strikes reciprocal chords in his audience. Similarly, his body becomes a 'thing', operating at a distance. In fact, it becomes the 'real thing' as far as Melba is concerned, and after an acquaintance of several minutes she determines on marriage. Nonetheless, she does take the precaution of handing a huge wad of money to Gus, her ex-husband, and instructs him to take his find and 'mature him up' before the prescribed wedding day.

Maturity, like everything else, is purchased, and in this instance, Gus's conception of a paternal role is to take Malcolm to Madame Rosita's for the lady in question to 'break him in'. But before this particular ceremony transpires, Malcolm makes a last effort to assert himself, suggesting that perhaps tattoos would be more 'usual' an initiation. Though he has adopted the vocabulary of the 'contemporaries', his confused memories of his father still date him. Since that gentleman sported a tattoo somewhere about his person, Malcolm would dearly like to duplicate the family tradition. The gathering hints of the boy's 'martyrdom' are evident when Professor Robinolte, the tattoo king, imprints stigmatical emblems of manhood onto the boy's virgin flesh by means of sharp needles. But the 'artist' is amazed to find that his victim betrays no pain whatsoever. It is as if Malcolm's very body had been anaesthetised during his 'short long' life. The extraordinary sexual stamina he displays at Madame Rosita's suggests similarly that all feelings have vanished from the body that is able to perform the mechanical motions of love. Gus, on the other hand, never recovers from the needles that puncture his flesh and dies during Malcolm's award-winning exploits upstairs. Perhaps his death is a mysterious correlative of the inner disintegration brought about by his services to Melba, as if his beautiful body were a hollowed shell that finally collapses from within. At any rate, marriage seems to perpetrate an analogous act of vampirism upon Malcolm who visibly wastes away and finally dies from his ritual enactment of *that one thing*, as Melba unerringly describes their love-making.

During this last phase of his career, Malcolm redistributes the clichés he has assimilated from the speech around him with an unknowing accuracy. For example, he tells Madame Girard in the course of one of their largely incoherent telephone conversations that he likes marriage very much, 'though it took a great deal out of him'. Purdy frequently satirises clichéd language by projecting literal equivalences in the hollow actions of those who use it. He conducts an attack upon the rigid patterning and prescription of experience by his own subtle exaggerations and parodies. Clichés are woven into ironic structures that restore a sense of the dynamic and mysterious relationships between words and experience. This is seen when Malcolm has his last dream-like confrontation with a 'father'. He and Melba are in a night club one evening when he is roused from his now habitual alcoholic stupor by the sight of a 'middle-aged unemphatically distinguished man, who might have posed for sparkling water advertisements', heading in the direction of the lavatory. The man is a walking cliché and, indeed, Melba assures the youth that the apparition was 'nobody's father', adding that anyway fathers have been 'old hat' for years. Malcolm's dazed insistence that 'he looked like him to a T' is quashed by the rejoinder that 'Millions of men look like millions of men, especially Americans'. But ironically, we suspect that this really ought to be Malcolm's father. 'Sparkling water' conjures up the youth's formless purity, his favourite drink of the hotel days and his murmuring sea-shells. Furthermore, Malcolm has been effectively reduced to (or obliged to remain) a *nobody*. (It should come as no surprise when his coffin is later rumoured to contain *no body*.) There is much sardonic humour as the boy assails and struggles to unmask the 'real thing', only to be accused of pederasty by his reluctant sire! Since this is a title he had heard applied to Mr Cox, Malcolm eagerly explains that he should not be confused with the gentleman. On the arrival of his old friend the policeman, he declares that anyhow pederasty is an honorific state only to be acquired after lengthy perusal of the stars. Once more he unwittingly exposes the moral vacuum that lies beneath the web of words; the venerable study of the heavens would appear to be the cover for another form of worship. Thus there are no fathers, only confidence men.

Adulthood has also come under a taboo in Melba's stardom and she becomes the 'Mama' of a 'white-haired angel boy'. Malcolm's traumatic loss of faith following his 'father's' refusal to be recognised has changed his hair to a miraculous white. It heralds his imminent return to the realm of 'sparkling waters'. Appropriately, his eventual death is the subject of as many contradictory theories and speculations as his life had been. According to Mr Cox, marriage proved fatal in his case, as in many others; the Cuban valet prefers to attribute it to pneumonia, whereas the physician diagnoses the combined effects of acute alcoholism and sexual hyperaesthesia (it is interesting to note that one meaning of the latter word is 'exaggerated aestheticism'). Melba, on the other hand, entertains no theories at all, having taken a drug to prevent her feeling any inconvenient emotion—perhaps a superfluous precaution on her part. There is nothing certain about the moment of death even. Madame Girard's prurient interest in Melba's extra-marital pastimes denies her the satisfaction of some last word. But Malcolm's departure from language has been a constant process, in some ways the only story of his life. To underline this, we are told that one of his last activities had been to commit to paper everything he could remember of his past conversations. Ironically, he finds it easier to record these in French as if this were somehow less 'foreign' than his 'adopted' tongue. Thus his last rites are to unburden himself of all the false words that had denied his potential as the hopeful spirit of love and thwarted his connections to some terrestial being.

His funeral is described in a manner which recapitulates the technique of simultaneously suggesting and destroying meanings, implicit in the 'texture' of the narrative as a whole. Madame Girard stage-manages the event as a 'command performance', but despite the grandiloquent deposits of flowers: 'She was greatly displeased, almost annihilated, however, that there was a ketchup factory in the nearby vicinity, and since the ketchup season was at its peak at the time of Malcolm's funeral, the burned saccharine smell of tomatoes struggled desperately with the evanescent perfume of violets and roses.' This sums up the manner in which Malcolm's fragile purity has been drowned in the sickly richness of society's 'sauces'. All gradations of youth and age are obliterated by the workings of a world whose motto might well be: 'Ripeness is all.' The passage implies that recourse to disguises and cosmetics of all kinds with which characters fashion artificial images of life, an 'exaggerated aestheticism' typified by Kermit's frenzied sprinkling of his studio with patchouli oil and rose water—Madame Girard's 'sine qua non' for habitations. The ultimate flaw in the funeral proceedings is, of course, the persistant rumour that there had been no corpse at all. Naturally, Madame Girard's version is 'full of evasions'.

Malcolm's story might seem to spring from King Lear's terrible words—'nothing will come of nothing', in that it concerns itself with the dissolution of those 'holy cords' that bind parent to child, person to person. Although its mode is that of irony, it projects similar inversions of the natural order. The novel charts a world where egoistic dynasties have mushroomed in the place of mutual responsibilities, where relationships have given way to power struggles and people to giant stars around which their dwarf-like victims orbit as empty satellites. Its landscape oscillates between the glittering palace and the dark closet and its dominant image is that of the circle. The latter is fixed in our minds by a sardonic imitation of the conventional dénouement. The last page gives us a brief résumé of the subsequent careers of the main protagonists and . . . the circles they continued to move in.

2

The Nephew

In contrast to the recurring image of the abandoned or orphaned child and his desperate search for identity in a fatherless world, other stories in the collections *Color of Darkness* and *Children is All* depict the relationship between mother and child. As already suggested, the father is frequently an elusive, shadowy figure, distinguished more by his absences than anything else. The mother, however, is emphatically present in her fight to prevent the child's attempts to fashion its own image and independence; she often seems to resist the natural process of growth and separation brought about by time, though this usually results in the intensification of the very rifts she seeks to counteract. Such a polarisation and severance of the parental bond has its own poetic logic, for if Purdy's work is viewed in overall terms as developing the notion that we are too often 'missing' from our own 'biography', then his first novels and stories can be understood as an attempt to trace this latter phenomenon to its roots and to chart its psychic ancestry. The absence of love has its counterpoint in a variety that is blind and sometimes devouring in its effects and the individual human soul, in its quest for maturity, is seen to have to negotiate between such extremes.

The qualities of maternal love have their purest rendering in the story 'Eventide', included in the collection *Color of Darkness*. Mahala mourns the departure of her son, Teeboy, whom she has lost to the adult world of jazz clubs and women friends. Those around her are quiet in the face of her grief—'what was there to say about a boy who had been practising to leave home for so long. Everyone had known it but her blind mother love.' Only when her son was just a baby had Mahala known perfect happiness; her love was fixed in the possessive vein of this first phase of mother-hood and since then she closed her eyes to Teeboy's growing away from her. In fact, he had gone 'missing' long before she was obliged to acknowledge the fact officially. Even then her recognition was equivocal . . .

> 'My Teeboy,' she would say, like the mother of a dead son, like the mother of a son who had died in battle, because it hurt as much to have a son missing in peacetime as to have lost him through war.

Having invested her life in idealised images of her son, his inevitable turning to the outside world is felt as the loss of her vital self—in such a case it is the mother who takes on the guise of the abandoned child. Her sister, Plumy, who has trailed through the city's infernal heat to seek news of the runaway, returns to tell her that he has straightened his hair and taken up with a white woman. Broken and empty, Mahala thus finds herself envying Plumy's own grief for a son who had died in childhood—there was a compensatory finality and perfection about his memory that time could never tarnish. The two women are locked in their separate pain. In a telling image of her reverence for the past and her ignorance of the inner self that has escaped old definitions, Mahala kisses the discarded clothing of her son. Plumy, meanwhile, is tortured by a fleeting vision of her dead boy. There is hope of a new intimacy between them, though, for her sister's distress moves Mahala to a compassionate recognition of the freshly smarting grief she has scarcely acknowledged until now. They sit together in the darkening room where time has stopped and where, like the flowers called four o'clocks that open at dusk to release their store of perfume, memory begins to unfold its healing idealising powers. They will cocoon themselves in 'sweet memory talk', to use the words of Mamie, a character in the story 'You Reach For Your Hat'. The last lines of 'Eventide' put a seal on the place where they will now dwell . . .

> the evening which had for some time been moving slowly into the house entered now as if in one great wave, bringing the parlour into the heavy summer night until you would have believed day-light would never enter there again, the night was so black and secure.

The mother is seen as a creator in more than a literal sense; she is portrayed simultaneously as an example of the universal endeavour to impose one's own pattern on the raw materials of existence. 'Cutting Edge', another story from this collection, deals more explicitly with the mother's aspirations to her legendary role of all-powerful matriarch. Whereas Teeboy's absence ultimately allowed Mahala to salvage her own image of him, the return of Bobby Zeller with his newly grown beard from New York to his parents' home in Florida shatters his mother's placid recollections of her son. In contrast with the previous story, the tone, as the title suggests, is sharp and incisive. The image of a blade is apt in a situation where a family is torn apart by the compulsion to carve and shape the self of another.

Mrs Zeller's absurd sense of outrage carries the seeds of prophecy: ' "But why a beard for heaven's sake," she cried, as though he had chosen something permanent and irreparable which would destroy all that they were.' The shock undermines the matriarchal grip and for a moment the mother is surprised to hear herself conversing freely in response to Bobby's chance remark concerning a servant girl his father is thought to have had an affair with. Memories invade her mind until she manages to check this involuntary frankness and reassert her inflexible opposition to her son's 'growth'. There is a further affront to her established rule when her husband initially refuses to appeal to his son, an act of insubordination which reminds her of his last attempted revolt over the question of the servant girl, Ellen Whitelaw, some twenty years previously. The final challenge to her supremacy comes when her son ostentatiously sunbathes naked in the garden. She feels annihilated.

Although the bitter conflict within the family is ostensibly over the question of Bobby's beard, it soon becomes clear that the comic piquancy of such a dispute cloaks more fundamental issues. The defiant beard expresses his desire to fashion his own image and is a reminder of his new-found status as an adult. In the same way, his sunbathing in the nude has the air of a calculated flaunting of his maturity. The gesture underlines his determination to act 'nakedly' as a frank, independent person, to discard constricting roles. He counters his father's eventual capitulation to his wife's tyranny with a refusal to play the part of a little boy. The reminder that this is the first request his father has ever made of him only incenses him further, since he feels that the rarity of such demands is at the root of the present troubles. Whereas Bobby asserts the naturalness of personal evolution, time seems to have passed his parents by. Mrs Zeller can accept no relaxation of her 'creative' powers whilst Mr Zeller is 'a man who kept everything down inside of him, everything had been tied and fastened so long, there was no part of him anymore that could struggle against the strictures'. Bobby despairs at his father's abdication and his willingness to preserve a semblance of domestic harmony at the price of such ossification. He is filled with contempt and pity by his child-like pleading to be spared the repetition of the six months' silence that was meted out to him over the case of the servant girl. He reflects that 'They were both young people who had learnt nothing from life, were stopped and drifting where they were twenty years before with Ellen Whitelaw.' Defeated and depressed by such intransigence, he attempts to extricate them from their deadlock by sacrificing the contentious beard. But even this is in vain as he realises the 'growth' will still be visible to them, despite the gashes and wounds he inflicts upon himself. The son's relegation to the status of a stranger is the outcome of his parents' own estrangement from the necessary movement of life.

Purdy is adept at conveying the modulations of perception that occur when stable notions of another's reality are subjected to bewildering fluctuations and reversals. Ordinary situations are suddenly shot through with intimations of a shadowy netherworld that threatens the familiar contours of relationships. His descriptions convey a peculiar tension between the pathetic and painful nature of breakdowns in communication and their more comic aspects. For example, the ominous noises that issue from Bobby's bedroom are said to silence his parents as effectively as if he were 'a wealthy relative who had commanded them never to question him or interfere with his movements even if he were dying'.

The power of empathy might be expected to develop, if anywhere, in the closeness of family relationships. In this author's analysis, however, the sanctified domain is stripped of its outward sentimentality. At its worst, it propagates the seeds of isolation and the child's predicament is too often a sad rehearsal of what awaits him in the outside world. In seeking to emasculate her menfolk, Mrs Zeller posits one extreme of the mother figure but by no means the definitive version. Others are portrayed as struggling to recognise their children's needs, even if the efforts to promote their welfare involve them in the kind of sacrifices Mrs Zeller exacts in others. In the collection *Children is All*, stories such as 'Night and Day' and 'Encore' recreate the crises that overtake two such women.

Cleo, in the first of these, is made to choose between a life of security and affluence with the grandfather of her child and one of impoverished uncertainty if she prefers her son. 'Grandy' is determined that she return the child to his errant son for the baby is a constant reminder of his own advancing years and the very manifestation of his proper relationship to Cleo. His desire for his daughter-in-law is bound up with fears of old age, he wants to usurp the place of his son as if to regain his own youth. Cleo spurns the cruel bargain once she has seen him for what he is— 'an old goat on his last legs'—to chance the future alone with her child. Merta, in 'Encore', in some ways illustrates the poignant consequences of such a choice. Similarly abandoned by her husband, she has fought to provide a home for her son, Gibbs. But having spent her best years slaving all hours in a factory, she is crushed by the realisation that her boy is practically friendless. The fruits of sacrifice are bitter. He is a nobody in their snob-ridden small town. He tries to escape the burden of her grieving love by frequenting a Greek family who are likewise outcasts by the town's criteria. In his despair at her interrogations, Gibbs tentatively begins to explain his isolation; he had never been invited to join a fraternity because—'You have to be rich at that college. And your parents have to be . . .' Merta cannot bear to hear nor can her son bear to tell his story. There are no words that can explain or subdue her suffering and the concluding image is of the mother begging the youth to keep on playing a tune on his harmonica, to drown out the discords within her.

'How wouldn't I know my own flesh and blood,' exclaims Edna, the central character in the play *Children is All*. Though she speaks of her son, Billy, expected home after fifteen years in the penitentiary for his part in a bank fraud, the words also anticipate her failure to know herself. The focus of attention is upon the efforts of Billy's ageing mother to reconcile herself to the home-coming of her criminal son. She worries that she will fail him due to her old feelings of shame and disapproval and though these fears are temporarily assuaged by the support of Leona, her friend, and the local pastor, her confidence fades away as the expected time for Billy's arrival comes and goes. It is whilst she is voicing her re-newed apprehensions that he slips into the room, unseen in the darkness, to overhear her. He has incurred a severe head wound in his break-out from prison and is to die unrecognised in his mother's lap as she goes through the motions of attending to his injury. All the while she stubbornly insists to those around her that he is a total stranger, though she will concede that his coming has miraculously pacified her troubled mind.

The play combines the different facets of maternal love seen in the preceding stories to dramatise a sacrifice of 'flesh and blood' that echoes the crucifixion of Christ. Purdy's work often incorpor-ates biblical allusions, stirring ironically within the text like memories just beyond recall and intimating that the ideals them-selves are all but forgotten. The penitentiary is a central image; its several connotations of imprisonment, penance and repentance lend an inner coherence to events. As the play progresses, it be-comes clear that the thirty-three year old Billy has been obliged to suffer not only for his own sins but for those of others. He has been made a sacrificial victim and is doubly imprisoned by the fact that his emotional development has been arrested by his mother's rejection of him. His break-out is motivated by the craving for forgiveness and acceptance. Edna has forged her own penitentiary and is unable to atone for her part in sin. She is convinced that Billy's home-coming must be the result of some official 'pardon' and cannot see that the authority he obeys is his love for her. The play's final tableau bears an ironic relation to the image of the Virgin Mary cradling the dead Christ. Unlike the archetype of idealised motherhood, Edna can only go through the motions of a grieving love. Yet the outward resemblances are revealing; Billy's mother has remained virginal in the sense that she has been un-touched by the crucial events in her life and the strangeness of her son is a measure of her remoteness from her *own* flesh and blood. Furthermore, her love is an ideal one too, but its abstract purity can only be maintained by a terrible sacrifice of sight, knowledge and ultimately of the very body she has launched into being.

Our understanding of her failure is built up gradually as the movement of the day underlines each stage in the psychic drama of her mind. There is a slow progression from dream to self-awareness, and to the blur of unconsciousness once more. Initially, Edna muses on the fretful night she spent thinking of her son and tells Leona, ominously enough, that with daylight she felt as if her eyelids were 'glued on'. In her dreams, Billy had pleaded with her to 'know' him when he returned, yet in her subconscious mind he has remained the little boy who came home on one occasion with a gashed brow for her to attend. Her confidence reaches its peak around noon when she is able to confront the fact that she was unable to help him during the various crises of adolescence and early manhood. She confesses further that she could never bring herself to visit him in prison, shrinking back at the very gates just as she recoiled from the shame of the courtroom when he badly needed her support to face the mass hostility of the assembled townsfolk. But as night falls and her son fails to appear, her confidence subsides once more.

Because of these revelations, considerable tension is generated as Edna fights to master her fears once and for all. She makes belated attempts to 'know' her son, to imagine how he will feel or how he will have changed. Ironically, Edna describes Billy as having always been 'late'—a word that accrues a specialised meaning in Purdy's work. It conjures up her disappointment at the world's tardiness to match her expectations of it, but also, the fact that within the play's emotional chronology it is Edna who is hopelessly 'late' to recognise her son. The pathos is sharpened by the 'total stranger's' obsessive need to receive proofs of her love and by the immediacy of his physical suffering. He actually resembles the wounded little boy his mother remembers of old. It is this recollection that fixes itself in Edna's distintegrating consciousness as she absent-mindedly dips her handkerchief in Billy's blood.

It would be a mistake to imagine that Purdy singles out the figure of the mother with the spite of an iconoclast, for the variety of maternal love that brings destruction in its wake is viewed with compassionate understanding, as well as awe. Furthermore, it is nearly always a concomitant of the father's 'abdication' and there is no bias against a particular sex. Though his women are convincingly real and individualised, it should be obvious that they are also fascinating in their more immediate relation to the process of *creation*—a concept, which in all of its ramifications, can be seen as a unifying preoccupation in his work. If the preceding material deals with the age-old disasters that overtake creation in terms of the relationship between the mother and child, the questions such images give rise to are woven into a metaphysical fable in the play *Cracks*. It employs the mode of an ironic allegory to describe how the rapport between an old woman and an orphaned child is interrupted by an encounter with the Creator himself, after he has made an unsuccessful attempt to bring to an end the miserable failure he considers his world to have been.

Despite her eighty years, which have rendered her child-like in some respects, Nera has taken on the responsibility of an infant abandoned by a neighbour. Unlike the previous play, extreme age and childhood are shown to have positive affinities. Both are stages where the imagination seeks to comprehend the enigmatic realm that lies on either side of life. From the perspective of age, life is rendered doubly perplexing if it has failed to define itself in meaningful antithesis to the gnawing fear of an encompassing nothingness. This is especially so in the case of Nera whose life-history, flouting verisimilitude, catalogues the workings of some manichean force. Her mother was left to scrub floors by a wealthy brother, her own four children died one after the other before reaching maturity and her husband, a petty embezzler, deserted her. In fact, she tells her nurse that one has to have troubles in order to speak at all, a pronouncement which is ironically confirmed by the revelation that the aforesaid brother who made and enjoyed twenty fortunes found his most desperate need to communicate after a stroke had paralysed and deprived him of the very faculty of speech.

In such a manner, the semi-naturalistic mode of some of the previous material is stripped away until we receive the impression of an almost abstract confrontation between life's potential and the disillusionment of old age. The child is present mainly as a voice which interrupts and utters a gnomic commentary on

Nera's flow of thoughts. Sometimes he quotes from a book that fascinates him by its references to 'cracks' and 'zephyrs of death' or he punctuates Nera's reminiscences with cries of joy or dismay at the opening and closing of the cracks he imagines in his bedroom walls. Elsewhere, Nera muses that she too was afraid of the 'cracks', or the 'ghosts' as she called them as a child. The word takes on further associations when she imagines what would have been the child's future if she had allowed him to be sent to an institution. Doctors and nurses, she cries, 'look on the body as an interesting mistake . . . no love in the world. Yes, the child is right about the cracks.' Life spilling from its cracked mould, flawed by the deficiency of love, is one facet of the image. Later, Nera's voice meanders through the night's immense silence, still tormented by the 'sharp piece of glass' in her brain . . .

> I have suffered nearly all the usual afflictions and bereavements . . . I lost everybody I loved, and now I'm waiting to join them if there is such a thing as an afterlife . . . I'm of two minds about it . . . In the late evening, if I'm comfortably tired and if the sky is beautiful and mild with stars and planets in easy view, I'm sure there must be more ahead . . . But often when I awake in a stiff posture in the morning, and my milk isn't brought to me by nurse, and the child is complaining and crying, I feel there's nothing after this life . . . And yet it's all so without sense that way . . . There has to be more to make this terrible life have meaning . . . It can't just stop here, that would be unfair.

Yet her words come just *after* the Creator has put an end to the world in a moment of despair which seems to endorse her view of life's bewildering futility. With much irony, the Creator is obliged to confess his inability to answer her 'haunting questions', for not only has she escaped his desire to put an end to Creation, thus enjoying the very afterlife she is in the process of doubting, but the questions she poses are those that have led him to despair. Disregarding his gentle reminders that everything is over, Nera pursues her quest for knowledge, pondering over the meaning of maternity and the pain of giving birth if it was all to come to nothing. Then, from her very depths, she utters the words—'Eternal, renewing itself, coming to itself again and again long after the pain of giving birth . . .' In a manner reminiscent of the child, she finds herself answering her own questions, as if quoting from some

51

mysterious book of life. In listening to her reverie, the Creator becomes aware that like her he has set in motion a force greater than himself. Her continued existence is a measure of this, but it is the indefinable qualities of her voice more than her actual words that renew his faith. Nera's account of childbirth articulates his own doubt over Creation, but she makes him see it as an act that transcends self to issue into being a perpetually renewed promise that cannot be negated by the suffering involved. The old woman maintains a stoic refusal to accept the finality of her own experience and displays a reverence before the mystery of life and death. The child's existence and her ability to offer him 'living love' for a while is all that matters. Whereas the image of childhood in the previous play denoted an arrested development, Nera's faith helps restore the literal meaning to the overall title of this collection— *Children is All*.

The allegoric vein is held in check by the wry humour of the situation. There is a comic aspect to many of Nera's speeches, as, for example, when she asks the Creator whether he hasn't escaped from some institution. At another point, she laughs aloud at the thought that the nurse and the child will never believe she has spent the whole night talking about 'nothing' with a total stranger. Yet in the full context, this 'nothingness' is seen to be all that is usually ignored by those in the midst of life; it is the realm of metaphysical speculation which insinuates itself through the 'cracks' in the fabric of everyday living. The humour also draws our attention to the importance of voices; their qualities are often more enlightening than the actual words spoken. Nera is moved to compliment the Creator on his beautiful voice and it is what she remembers most from their conversation—the substance of his remarks as regards the end of the world are quite ignored. The paradox that torments her is understood and expressed in an analogous way; the mysterious words that arise in her consciousness are like the pure sound of life itself, springing free of its material forms to reassert its magic potency. The play's overall construction reinforces this effect. The 'content' of Nera's story is established with the minimum of elaboration so as to concentrate our attention upon the very sound of those cadences common to us all when we address ourselves to the old woman's questions . . . 'Where are we going?' and 'Will we live for ever?'

Purdy's second novel, *The Nephew* (1961), was published a year before the stories and plays brought together in *Children is All* and in some ways it anticipates the two extremes of motherhood depicted in the figures of Edna and Nera. But whereas the plays isolate dramatic images of the mysteries of destruction and creation, the novel form allows the author to convey the minute accretions of knowledge that mark the stages of Alma's journey between these two poles. On the surface, this second novel seems quite simple and straightforward in its narrative structure: Alma Mason, a retired school teacher who lives with her brother, Boyd, a real-estate agent, embarks on the writing of a 'memorial' of her young nephew, Cliff, so as to occupy her mind during the period of anxiety brought on by a telegram informing them that he is missing in action in the Korean War. The aged couple care deeply about the boy for they had shared their home with him, after his parents had been killed in a plane crash. Alma's search for material leads her to seek assistance from neighbours and others in the locality who had known her nephew. It is a task which brings her to a reappraisal of the lives around her, though the project itself never materialises due to the puzzling nature of the information she discovers. Ultimately, official word comes through to confirm Cliff's death and Alma puts the memoir aside to find solace in a new understanding and companionship with her brother.

Summarised in such a fashion, the framework of events would seem to serve primarily as a basis for the painstaking evocation of the life-style of a sleepy quarter of a small American town. Such a reading would single out the novel's naturalistic effects for praise, since it conjures up the very spirit of the place through its documentation of the trivia of domestic life, neighbourhood traditions and routines and so engages in a wry observation of the local residents and their idiosyncracies. The narrative is steeped in the idioms of the small town, much of it being made up of conversation in a homely and colloquial vein which is both amusing and life-like. There is endless talk of gardens, home-cooking and the relative merits of property, there are many frissons over the progress of local scandals. In short, the bizarre happenings, extraordinary characters and satirical style of *Malcolm* seem to have been left behind completely.

Yet even as the product of a cursory reading such an approach is unsatisfactory; there are too many points at which the text seems to resist the interpretative code that would seek to categorise the novel within the genre of the 'small town study'. All the paraphernalia of material reality, the gestures, dialogues and other descriptive residues seem to be surcharged with something more than a straightforward mimetic function. Words such as 'missing', 'memorial', 'doubt' and 'belief' form curious motifs and seem to belong to some other axis of order. Many conversations are contextualised in a fashion that directs our attention to the choice of vocabulary a character will employ as if it were almost more important than the content of speech. Such enigmas challenge the reader to structure his perception along more complex lines and provoke the feeling that some 'inner text' will be revealed. The same impression haunts Alma with regard to the written communications she receives from or about the nephew. For example, she handles one of his letters with great care as if it might suddenly disclose a second sheet of stationery—perhaps that 'real' letter she dreams of. Or when the telegram arrives to inform her that the boy is missing, we are told—'The casual and empty wording of the message for a moment did not convey to her the dreadfulness of the import . . . like Cliff's letters, the "content" did not quite come through, and she was left with the impression that a more complete message would soon be on its way.' Alma is like that hypothetical reader posited by the naturalistic version of the novel sketched above. She had thought of herself as moving in a realm that had long appeared familiar and perfectly comprehensible to her, yet we are made to share the gradual clouding of those once clear-cut dimensions as the cosy, small town world is rent by the 'cracks' that had obsessed Nera and her child, to reveal a mysterious infrastructure.

Another approach might be prompted by the recognition of the now familiar convention of the 'novel within the novel'. In other words, we would seek to locate that hoped for 'inner text' by the way in which Alma's projected biography affords an examination of the artist's interaction with his material. Yet her difficulties as a 'reader' are matched by those she experiences as an aspiring 'writer'; the portrait she wishes to compile is fractured by ambiguities and Cliff might almost be the elusive spirit implicit in the town's name—'Rainbow Centre'—for his tangible self seems nowhere in existence. The 'memorial' is oddly true to its name, it houses nothing. The novel's circularity also seems to underline Alma's failure as a writer; it opens and closes on Memorial Day but on this second occasion the flag she and Boyd were wont to hang out is in pieces. The fate of Old Glory appears to serve as an appropriate epitaph on the material content that 'did not quite come through' for when Alma seeks to repair it—'the tear was not so easily repaired, she saw, once she began working over it. Other long-hidden snags and rents in the material suddenly asserted themselves, as if in conspiracy with the first rent in the fabric, and soon Alma saw that what she held was a tissue of rotted cloth, impossible to mend.'

Ultimately then, perhaps in exasperation, one might want to relegate the novel to the ranks of those that flaunt their own autonomy and exult in their ability to destroy the very meanings they suggest—a type that is at its most subtle in a work like *Les Gommes* by Alain Robbe-Grillet. But although Purdy might reflect upon the philosophic implications of his craft as much as the practitioners of the *nouveau roman*, he doesn't indulge in aesthetic acrobatics for their own sake and is less willing to forgo the novel's traditional engagement with spiritual values. His interest in the fate of words in a commercialised culture stems from a revulsion that they should be harnessed to de-humanising ends and he leads us to an identification of similar dislocations at the level of ordinary relationships. It is an approach to language that bears an interesting relation to Plato's idea that writing ought to be condemned for its severance of the word from the communicative presence which alone could be the source of meaning and truth. The proposition illuminates a process of loss which in Purdy's analysis takes place more regrettably within individuals. It is particularly apposite in the case of Alma and her struggle to unlearn the reflex to 'write'. The author should not be misconstrued as subscribing literally to Plato's doctrine; rather than taking the constitutive feature of verbal forms to be their inability to contain reality, he sees the occurrence as the *symptom* of some spiritual impoverishment at a deeper level. He is concerned in a more generic sense with the severance of meaning from a variety of forms, linguistic, literary or social, at the point where they have become mere 'memorials' of the spirit they claim to house. Almost in the manner of a semiologist, he often seems to investigate a transverse section of language. Certainly, Alma's involvement with the 'material' of her nephew's biography takes the shape of a belated initiation into the complexities of the indices that surround her in all her relationships. Approached in this light, the novel no longer charts her humiliating defeat. On the contrary, Alma is seen to arrive at the 'Threshold of Assent' (as the last chapter is entitled) where she transcends her former desire to use words to construct a falsehood. Her assent to silence and her acceptance of life's mysteries does not imply the futility of language systems. It is a silence to which the 'communicative presence' has been restored, one of plenitude, not emptiness, and one from which words do arise, bathed in new qualities to express her love. Despite her *artistic* failure, the encompassing novel (which does get written!) springs from the viewpoint Alma has attained and itself constitutes that inner biography not only of her nephew but also of his aunt and the others for whom he had meaning.

At the beginning of the narrative Alma belongs in spirit to the world of the naturalistic novel where the illusion of material reality is complacently self-sufficient. Through her the genre is subtly parodied for its 'omissions'. Alma has ordered her life and those around her with few doubts as to the propriety of her conduct. She has surrounded herself by her 'things'; she cares for her properties, even purchasing a neighbouring house at a mean price only to have it pulled down so as to afford a better view of the sunset, and occupies her spare time by supervising her investment in a gift shop that sells souvenirs. She has retained the inflexible mannerisms of the schoolmarm and her voice knows only the modulations of authority. Boyd is bossed and mothered; their relationship has hardened into a fixed shape, ordained by habit and routine and energised only by a scarcely dissimulated mutual exasperation. For example, Alma absorbs the image of him chewing custard pie with his mouth open 'as if to take in the full unsightliness of his table etiquette and, armed with this vision, be even firmer with him in the future'. But her sense of an underlying loss in the reality of this little world is evident by her anxious scrutiny of the nephew's letters. She prides herself on the particularity of her rapport with Cliff, confident that she thinks of him far more than Boyd does and convinced that her brother's prosaic mind is unable to grasp the real import of these communications. Despite the fact that the letters are paltry and insipid, that they *say* almost nothing at all—'It was in the little they said that Alma read the much that was there. It was in Cliff's omissions that she saw his life.' A kind of infinite regression is set in motion in that physical separation is followed by the failure of language to bridge that gulf and then by the prophetic irony of the telegram establishing Cliff's status as a 'missing person'. But as Cliff recedes in one direction, Alma and Boyd, because of the ever increasing volume of words which 'apostrophise' him in his absence, move off in contrary fashion.

It is also made clear that whilst the nephew had in fact been living with the couple, they had both been *away* for much of the time, Boyd off on his business deals and Alma teaching school in a neighbouring town. The present is brought into sharper focus by these disclosures from the past. In both cases, physical separation coincides with a deeper alienation. The sense of emptiness, of life passing by just out of reach, is compensated for (and paradoxically intensified by) the shaping of fictions that depend upon that distance. The pathos of this process is conjured up deftly by the description of the old couple in their 'specially prepared darkness':

> As they talked to one another in the dark, it even seemed to them that they were living their entire lives all at once, and were in command of their total personalities. Friends and relatives long dead entered into their conversation, and the hard implacable void of contemporaneity was dissipated. One could, so to speak, see land, breathe air. The night had lifted from night.

In a similar vein, the image of Cliff that Alma 'reads' between the lines of his letters is constructed out of the desired view of herself as a loving surrogate parent. But this aspect of herself has never been expressed, just as Boyd has never had the son he yearns for. Alma and Boyd are the ones who are really 'missing'—their 'biographies' do not contain these inner selves and Cliff embodies that spirit of life which they falsify and maintain at a distance through their refusal to 'know' him. His 'official' disappearance has the effect of a subterranean shock upon the secret investment of their ideal self image in him. It is as if hope dies within them and they become their true age, though neither will admit to this onset of doubt.

Appropriately, it is the word 'missing' itself that starts off the chain of reactions that is to lead them to re-possess and bring 'home' those inner selves that have been banished. But before this can happen, they are obliged to submit to a painful process of discovery about themselves and about other people. This is rendered largely through the emphasis upon their language and its problematic relation to 'reality', to Cliff, and to what is missing from their lives. The enigmatic telegram forces them to become aware of the difficulties of weighing up words and implants the suspicion that language might be used to 'cover up' rather than to impart meanings. This dawning intuition is uneasily measured against their own speech, as the following conversation makes clear . . .

For some time after Cliff had been reported missing, Alma had allowed Boyd the freedom to say that *he didn't know, just didn't know*, until one evening, at the beginning of summer, putting down the *Sentinel*, she said with great sternness and force:

'I don't know why in heaven's name you keep saying *you don't know* when it is perfectly clear that you think he won't return.'

'That's not what I think at all. Not by a long shot,' he replied, both wounded and incensed. 'As usual, you're jumping to conclusions before you see the evidence.'

'I *know* he'll be back!' she cried, in the same tones she employed in her political and religious arguments.

'I know you do,' Boyd said in his most conciliatory manner, placing the argument now likewise in the arena of the historical and objective. 'But when I say *I don't know*, I mean just that.'

'Fiddle,' she said with real anger.

'I don't know, Alma,' he told her, and he shook the pages of the *Sentinel*.

'You have a feeling one way or another. Everybody does.'

'How like a woman,' he shook his head.

'You have your own feeling, which is stronger in one direction or another, and being a man or woman has nothing to do with it. Everybody who thinks or feels knows what he thinks or feels about someone's being missing or not missing, going to return or not going to return.'

'All right, all right,' Boyd bent under her attack.

'I know you think Cliff's not coming back,' Alma said, and her voice broke.

Though as yet unaware of what she is actually doing, we can infer two processes at work in Alma. Firstly, and with her habitual belligerence, she is trying to eradicate her own unacknowledged doubt by projecting it upon Boyd (whom she describes elsewhere as leaving so much to be desired). She wants to impose her version of events upon him. But simultaneously, she seeks desperately to penetrate the surface of his words, as if to entertain at second hand the possibility of the feelings she represses, half-realising that it is what is *not* said that might be important. The breaking of her voice points to the first tremulous questioning of the part of herself that 'delivered the speeches' and which had previously functioned autonomously.

The machinery that 'delivered the speeches' had always run smoothly on the raw material provided in ample quantities by the failings of Alma's neighbours. As with those fiction-making so-phistries that efface Cliff, it is the distance that she is careful to maintain between herself and adjoining lives that enables her to preserve their 'stories' intact and neatly inventoried in the annals of her mind. It is not surprising to find that one of her favourite remarks is that she likes to be surrounded always by her own property. The combined plights of Mrs Van Tassel and her drunken lodger, of Faye Laird's submission to the tyranny of her senile mother, and of Willard Baker, the dissolute and ageing scion of a 'front' family with a particularly awesome history, afford Alma the comfort of casting pitying glances in their direction whilst deploring their immoderate recourse to some external support in their lives. (Minnie Clyde Hawke's walking cane with its ornate exterior forms a comic aside upon the generalised discrepancies between 'form' and 'meaning' since it conveniently conceals a brandy flask in its hollowed stem.) Each constitutes some special 'case' and the periodic installments of 'news' find a ready-made set of criteria by which they can be absorbed. Boyd, ironically, is of such 'solidified opinion' that he cannot even accommodate the minor adjustments that Alma, in her nicety, is willing to entertain. Brother and sister look at the world and 'read' its signs by their own arrested termin-ology. Alma, who always keeps a sharp look out for symptoms of

Clara Himbaugh's local proselytising, would impose her own stasis upon the neighbourhood, as if she were the self-appointed guardian of its moral fibre. She would perpetuate her dominion as schoolmarm, the arbiter of behaviour and the dispenser of knowledge.

But apart from her vast reserves of belligerence, Alma, an old maid, is comically unqualified to perform such universal motherhood. The irony is echoed in her name, with its intimations of 'Alma Mater', the benign mother figure—especially as her 'alumni' all signally refuse to acknowledge her as such. As Boyd is fond of pointing out, there is no end to her ignorance about the town, about people and life. With the accelerating sense of emptiness that follows Cliff's disappearance, Alma begins to *feel* the weight of such comments and muses now upon the adult problems of those around her with 'a growing sense of mystery and unease'. At the same time, drawn by her grieving to seek a rapprochement, her neighbours start to suspect that Alma is perhaps human after all, and prone to all the painfulness of that condition. Newly humbled and brooding over the dearth of her mail in contrast to the volumes that are observed to be delivered to the surrounding houses, she is unprepared for the shock of finding herself on the receiving end of Clara Himbaugh's ardent Christian Science. Her immediate reaction is to recoil in indignation from the 'strong "reader's" tones' that are addressed to her. It requires all her energies to quell the rebellious outbreak of well-meaning condescension. But despite her imperious looks and thunderous switches of subject in mid-conversation, she is unable to efface Clara's parting volley to the effect that she ought to occupy herself by writing down her memories of Cliff. As if of its own volition, the word 'memorial' springs to Alma's lips, and once said it remains to haunt her 'like a melody she had heard unwillingly and even more unwillingly remembered'. The seeds of doubt sown in Alma's psyche by the fateful telegram find a counterpart in the questioning looks that contradict her friends' 'dulcet words'. In spite of the battle she wages on all fronts to quash this subterranean language at birth, the enemy stirs from within as the term 'memorial' repeatedly slips past her conscious guard. Her subconscious, as if part of some more general conspiracy, compounds its infidelity by insistently coupling the word with the smell of cooking tomatoes that pervaded the town during the summer months. Soon, 'She hated the tone, the sound, the meaning of *memorial* as much as she did that of the ketchup, and the two, odour and word, were an exacerbation in her mind.' Few of the local inhabitants like to be reminded of the factory the town depended upon, nonetheless, for its livelihood—in itself an ironic confirmation of a wider refusal to recognise their addiction to all kinds of 'sauces' that obliterate what is felt to be unpalatable (recalling the ending of *Malcolm*).

To defuse those inherent associations with death, Alma attempts to shape the word to her own purposes, assigning it private meanings. The appropriation is launched by a somewhat embarrassed avowal to Boyd that she is toying with the notion of writing some sort of family record, the inference being that it is a mere whim on a par with her old enthusiasm for the gift shop. She conceals its ulterior purpose, that of testifying to her faith in Cliff's imminent return, assuring herself of their special relationship and documenting the basis upon which his future glories will provide her with the 'reward' of her life. Accordingly, a large black notebook is unearthed with RECORDS stamped impressively on its cover, as if heralding the business-like zeal of the undertaking. Yet her confidence melts away before the blank pages. Although a flood of unsuspected memories overtakes her, none of them seems quite 'tidy' enough to carry out her intentions. Alma's inability to write contrasts ironically with other examples of 'writing' in the novel as apparently innocuous details reorganise themselves esoterically around the central axis to discharge their wry humour. Her mother, for instance, had blessed the world with a 'memorial' to her culinary expertise which immortalises in 'firm precise hand-writing' the recipes that had been second nature to her. Elsewhere, Mrs Barrington is seen to rule the neighbourhood from her spinet writing desk by the summonses and edicts that flow from her 'model Spencerian hand'. With such women for alter egos, it is no wonder that the 'untidy' Cliff seems to escape all the categories into which Alma would place people. Yet as she suspends the determination to write *things* down, a new kind of perception unfolds. The puzzling welter of feelings that are unlocked constitute the first hesitant steps in a discovery of what was previously missing in her existence. One such sensation concerns the experience of time:

How odd, how terrifying, and yet how soothing, she thought, putting down the record book, that time runs out.

First we are here, she said to herself, being this sort of person and then so little later we have lost all track of that time and who we were then, until some trifle brings us back to that period for a brief lightning-illumined second, then back again to the now.

This burgeoning of memories contrasts with an earlier image of Alma where the desire to fix and dictate the content of a feeling in advance resulted in a blankness equalling that of her record book. When Cliff went off to the induction centre, his aunt gathered up all the clothes strewn around his room and 'holding them as carefully as if she wished not to lose all the folds and creases Cliff had left behind in them' deposited the pile in an immense cedar chest which was then locked. Ignoring the fact that the garments would never fit him again, Alma would not let herself reopen the box. She secretly rejoiced in the strange feeling of hope produced when her hand strayed over the wood's smooth surface. It is a poignant image of her blind love and the self-defeating ideal of exclusive possession. Alma can only hoard up empty *things* and caress surfaces beneath which the defining 'body' has fled. The treasure chest is more like a coffin. It is the reflex of motherhood seen in Mahala in the story 'Eventide' and Edna in the play *Children is All*, but it is also the metaphor of a universal failing, as Boyd amply demonstrates.

Boyd has helped to trap his sister in her puritan strait-jacket and like her he attempts to manipulate people according to some ideal version of them. Having always fastidiously cushioned her from whatever he considered to be 'unpleasant' (a category that ranged from her mother's terminal illness to Willard Baker's suspected homosexuality), he is irritated by her growing curiosity about the troubles of their neighbours as her grief turns its questioning gaze upon the face of the outer world. Their conversations become fraught with the weight of what is unsaid and are richly suggestive of the drama unfolding within Alma's psyche. Boyd almost takes on the role of her conscious guard, seeking to intercept anything that disturbs cherished conceptions. She is accused of living in and 'digging up' the past, as if he were incapable of accommodating more than the masquerade of daily 'news' from the pages of the *Sentinel*. Yet not only do Boyd's faulty manners stand in comic contradiction of the standards he imposes elsewhere, but the very words with which he would exorcise Alma's unwelcome researches rebound upon him too. Having commanded her to let their nephew 'rest in peace', he is obliged to wince as the secondary meanings overtake him.

But neither Boyd, Alma or their nephew are allowed to 'rest in peace'. Boyd, in particular, is obliged to follow his sister's stock-taking of the impoverishment that results from a preference for fictions. He too has a private 'memorial' of Cliff, one which is regarded as evidence of the latter's supposedly exclusive attachment to him. But the locked strong-box, containing the four thousand dollars mysteriously discovered on Cliff's person after the party at Willard Baker's to celebrate his departure for the army, is as eloquent of the doubts Boyd wanted to shut away, doubts which lie dormant like the proverbial skeleton in the cupboard. The community as a whole bristles with secrets and hidden alliances that have been cloaked by surface signs. Such phenomena bespeak the fragmentation of shared experience and knowledge that Alma, forced to recognise her dependence upon other people in the search for Cliff, must fathom and seek to reverse before her wounds can heal. She must puzzle over and piece together the interlocking parts of a new picture.

Lessons concerning the futility of trying to prescribe the future are served on her by various friends. Mrs Van Tassel, acceding reluctantly to a review of her lodger, is adamant in her refusal to renounce Minnie Clyde Hawke and the friendship that had begun to console both women in the loneliness of widowhood, merely to preserve Alma's notion of the desired tone of the neighbourhood. Her mention of the four thousand dollar loan that had initially brought them together carries the disquieting postscript that Alma had never been approached for assistance as she had always thought of her as 'away'. Faye Laird conducts a similar manœuvre in the face of a withering interrogation on the subject of Clara Himbaugh's ministrations to her mother, when she retaliates with the heretical suggestion that prayer might help to bring Cliff home too. As Alma had always to approve the contents of a discussion in advance, such losses of control introduce discomforting glimpses of the image other people hold of her—one which the proud concealment of her inadequacies, even from herself, has been unable to stem.

Her desire to know only the 'right things' is similarly confounded when she realises that the person most likely to hold the key to her nephew's biographical self is Professor Mannheim. In the past she put as much distance as possible between herself and such 'moral lepers' (even, one suspects, to the extent of buying and tearing down his adjoining property so that her immaculate panorama might be unspotted), but must now find a way of approaching the figure ostracised by the community for his political and sexual energies. Anxieties multiply when she ponders on the kind of information the Professor might supply her with: 'Cliff's biography—if he had one—was likely to consist of the very elements which a man would not be apt to tell a woman. Even supposing that the professor knew the elements, he might not be able to know or recognise the important ones—the real ones— in Cliff's life . . .' There are obvious ironies here in that the Professor indeed does know, and has recognised, some of the important experiences in Cliff's life, yet he is unlikely to confide them to Alma. Her comment reveals the impossibility of real communication by its characteristic determining of conclusions in advance of any evidence. Furthermore, it demonstrates in miniature the kind of thinking that has made him the victim of a trial by prejudice in the larger community.

Cliff, on the other hand, had few preconceptions about people, and whilst his aunt and uncle were 'away', he was cherished by other outsiders precisely because he was so open-minded and easy to talk with. Only during her flux of unsuspected memories had his aunt drawn near to this aspect of him in the feeling that— 'he possessed that astonishing fresh look, as if he had just come out of a forest, perhaps, or even a pond, still dripping a little from his bath', though sadly, even here, the imagery is of a wanderer from another world. As with Malcolm, there are intimations of some unrecognised divinity in Cliff, as if the dream-filled connections he has with most other people convey their failure to realise the potential of life. Though his disappearance coincides with their own vanished youth, the community seems to drift on in its self-administered timeless limbo, the character of which can be read in Faye Laird, who—'looked neither young nor old, middle-aged or mature. There was something of the midget in her face, not wrinkled enough for a woman of forty, and too worn for that of a child.' Furthermore, it is no accident that Cliff is revealed to be associated with the very people Alma and Boyd *ignored* and that his 'rehabilitation' is made to depend upon their forging links with the elements of life they had outlawed. The latter part of the narrative centres upon two contrasting attempts to gain an access to Cliff through such people. The first concerns the approach to Professor Mannheim via the intermediary of Mrs Barrington (Alma has been brought to see that the price she gave him for his house was so stingy that it now makes it difficult for him to be casually invited to cross her threshold), and the second involves Vernon Miller, whose gradual movement to the foreground of the novel denotes the eventual breakdown of Alma's false categories.

Mrs Barrington's role as intermediary brings out some of the finest humour in the novel. Her manner of intervention spells out the impossibility of attaining knowledge that has been implicit in all Alma's relations with people. Alma agrees that—'if Mrs Barrington asked anybody—especially a professor—to tell anything, it would be a royal command, and he'd have to tell whether he knew anything or not.' The 'old monarch' is eminently qualified to perform such a part since she translates Alma's characteristics onto an imperial scale—she is the 'transient spirit' of Rainbow Centre, glorying in her 'exits and entrances'. She roams the nation, despite the handicap of a 'missing' foot and the lack of a husband, who even when alive 'had played such an inconspicuous part in her life . . . that his actual death came like a mere corroboration to the public of the old suspicion that he had never existed at all'. Even during her absences she still manages to broadcast her superiority over lesser mortals by the tourist-drawing splendours of her paradisiac garden and its monumental trumpet vine. Before Mrs Barrington's help is solicited, Alma has a prophetic dream during the course of which she launches into a devastating critique of her revered neighbour—the bitter fruit of years of pent-up irritation. The whole of the imagined conversation is very funny, and its climactic moment is highly significant in terms of Alma's education. At the height of her invective, the quarry is cornered behind the redoubtable trumpet vine, but is unmasked only to reveal a more perspicacious version of herself:

Then quite unexpectedly as it might have done in real life, this imaginary conversation shot beyond the fore-knowledge of the imaginer.

'And Cliff, I suppose, is not one of your own things, as you put it,' Mrs Barrington's cold face came from behind the vine.

'You dare mention him in this connection.' Alma's voice was lower than her usual pitch for Boyd's accustomed level of hearing, but clear enough for Mrs B's.

'Very well, my dear. You began the argument—allow me to continue it. Cliff was as much to you in the way of one of *your* possessions, Alma, as my yard or my garden, my house or my trumpet vine, and while I have had the luxury of being able to talk about a good many of my *things*, I am afraid you have rather limited yourself to just the one subject.'

If Alma is forced to see her present self in Mrs Barrington, she is subsequently given a nightmarish vision of what her future could become in the person of old Mrs Laird. Faye's mother is in the final, decomposing stages of a life of tyranny, a match for the strongest applications of Christian Science, or for the spewing fantasies of the TV that diverts some of her attention from her daughter's incipient bestiality. Faye has been crippled by her subservience to her mother's will and endures the most cruel attacks ('If I hadn't watched her night and day years ago, she would have brought criminal disgrace on all of us. No control of her instincts!'). Alma's charitable intentions shrivel before a broadside that outstrips any of her own, and there is a certain amount of harsh justice for her to be addressed in her 'absence' as guilty of spending a lifetime bossing other people and, rather more wildly, to be accused of harbouring incestuous designs upon her brother, for which outrage she is now in jail.

Mrs Barrington conducts her *rule* in a more lucid fashion, having decided at an early age that since life had no intrinsic meaning, she would enforce her own. In accordance with these principles, Boyd is instructed that, if necessary, the whole community must help Alma to complete her 'memorial'—the logic being that its value lies in its execution as an act of will, regardless of its contents or the absurdity of the very idea. In other words, there must be a continuum in the persona Alma has created for herself, otherwise there is a danger she might 'dry up and blow away'. Such nihilistic philosophy translates itself into gesture, as when she 'indicated by a sudden rearrangement of herself on the sofa that the *why* of Alma's predicament did not need to occupy their attention'. This disregard for a person's inner self, for their emotional 'contents', is put into practice in the case of Professor Mannheim, a mere *name* to Mrs Barrington. He receives a magisterial summons to her court and is briefed on what is expected of him, though all the while Mrs Barrington's mind is elsewhere. The comic scene is also terrifying in its picture of the human dereliction that underlies the demure surface of conversation. Whilst Mrs Barrington is 'away' at the Elks where she is due to deliver a luncheon speech, the Professor is overcome by the strain of the interview which he had 'mis-read' as heralding the long-anticipated blow to his career —one that had consisted in a singular failure to meet the requirements of what his interlocutor 'thought a life long resident of Rainbow and the college campus should be'. Having finally grasped that Cliff was to be the subject of their discussion, he responds to the distance behind the request for information in commensurate fashion by offering some of his old papers and essays. Ironically, though, the memory of Cliff becomes associated with his secret preoccupation with the anniversary of his first wife's death, and is particularly meaningful to him because of the confidences he had shared with the boy and which had relieved him of suicidal thoughts. A flood of memories is unleashed incoherently, until they are broken by an outburst of animal-like sobs. But as real emotion fractures the surrounding artificiality, it elicits no reciprocal tremor in his audience. Though Alma is already disturbed by the whole situation, she allows Mrs Barrington's impassive demeanour to suppress her agitation. Mrs Barrington acts as though weeping were precisely what she had had in mind for the interview's termination.

Thus Alma's hoped-for enlightenment is aborted. Inevitably, the spirit in which the inquisition is conducted causes the Professor to withhold 'the only thing about him (Cliff) worth knowing'. Having been victimised in the past for speaking his mind, he is now careful to acquiesce outwardly to their restricted codes, and apart from his temporary loss of control, allows the situation to determine what can be said. His pathetic loneliness is reinforced when he tries to tell his wife about Cliff and the four thousand

dollars, for she can only regurgitate *names*—insisting that Vernon
Miller and Willard Baker are known 'homosexuals', as if the word
itself pre-empted the need for any further discussion. He is warned
that he must concentrate his energies on reaching the golden age
of retirement unscathed.

The oppressive cloud of Mrs Barrington's self-sufficiency lifts
with her subsequent departure. For Alma, it is like a reprieve from
the part of herself that had aspired to match her neighbour's iron
will. The investment of this self image in the 'memorial' (to the
irritating extent that it seemed 'publicly commissioned') has been
slowly erased by the continued blankness of its pages. The turning
point of the narrative comes when she puts it away 'gently, almost
finally' in a drawer. Alma is beginning to face up to the inadequacy of her knowledge of Cliff and her gesture is significant in
that it shows her resisting the temptation to 'write a story' that
would paint over the pain. She gratefully absorbs herself in the
humble tasks around the house and garden that needed her attention and, appropriately, it is whilst her artistic preoccupations are
in abeyance that she moves obliquely to an understanding of her
nephew. This takes place as the barriers she had erected between
herself and neighbours are eroded by the new spirit of tolerance
that wells from her meditative state. Like Boyd, there were some
things she had chosen to be deaf to, but now she welcomes the
sound of Willard Baker's voice, and wonders afresh on the tragedy
of his family. They exchange pleasantries and small talk until soon
Alma is glad to do him favours such as looking after his mail
during his vacation or even putting herself out to do some house-
work for him. Willard's frankness provides her with an example of
someone who can confess to a need for other people and to a lack
of self-sufficiency. He even jokes about his weaknesses, telling her
that he would have been ripe for Clara Himbaugh's proselytising
if Vernon weren't already his 'Christian Science'. He is also alert
to Alma's inner worries and broaches the subject of Cliff by revealing that Vernon knew him well. The force of this information is
dramatically realised when she and Boyd have to deal with a fire
that breaks out mysteriously in Vernon's locked room whilst he
and Willard are away. After the door has been broken open
with an axe, the old couple are struck with wonder as they see
that . . .

An almost life-sized series of photos of the nephew, stretched across the walls of the room by wires, raced giddily before them in the reflection and consummation of the fire. Why they had not seen the photographs at once, they did not know. Together with the flames and the hour of the night, Cliff seemed, burning in the conflagration of the room, about to speak, his one hand extended to them, as if in life, in an eloquent orator's gesture.

Alma and Boyd must face the fact that a stranger could have a private collection of 'pictures' of Cliff in the 'light' of which their own paltry stock of souvenirs (they can only find one small photograph of him) seems to be wiped out. When a telegram arrives soon afterwards to inform Alma that her nephew's death has been established, only to be followed by the news that there is nothing left of him to ship home, it might appear that his bodily disintegration echoes that other 'holocaust' which lays waste the images in Vernon's room and elsewhere, to finalise his 'absence'. Nevertheless, this double decomposition should not be seen as elegising the 'death' of meaning, or the impossibility of ever knowing another person. The novel does not culminate in such a bleak irony, and the two events can be understood more fully as delivering a last shock to the tenacious habit of hiding feelings behind a mask of self-sufficiency, one from which it never recovers. Such a removal of the inner self from the surface of life and from interaction with others has brought about its own petrification—the various images of Cliff that had been jealously secreted away are consumed by the manifest inadequacy of their claim to make him their exclusive property. However, just as the hiding away of these images and all that had been invested in them breeds doubt, so their resurrection to the play of consciousness and shared enquiry brings about an affirmation of belief in Cliff's innocence and goodness. This sharing of experience and the new willingness to use language to communicate rather than to cover up, allows the nephew, finally, to come 'home'.

In the case of Boyd, the shock takes the form of a heart attack. Yet not only does this allow him the luxury of giving up the specious movement that had characterised his past, to devote himself to those same small tasks that brought respite to Alma, but it also opens up another door to his sister that had used to be barred. Whereas her forced entry to Vernon's room had resulted only in incomprehension, because Vernon himself is still an unknown entity to her, with Boyd, she recognises with warmth and affection, the weaknesses he had tried to hide, and finds a new vocation in caring for him *openly*. Nor is she crushed by the fateful telegram, on the contrary, her friends are awed by the conversion of her old severity to a new inner strength that allows her simultaneously to drop her mask of infallibility. She struggles to confess to them that during her brother's illness—'when he was perhaps a bit beside himself, he called and called for his nephew. I had not realized until then how much Cliff had come to mean for him, you see. He was all the son Boyd felt he had . . . I think I realized then that it was Boyd who cared for him perhaps the most, while you see it was I who always talked and talked . . . and was going to write the book.'

After this convalescence, when it might appear that their old pattern of life would be resumed, Alma counters the first resurgence of fantasy when her brother chides her for not finishing the book. She surprises herself even, by asserting that the 'memorial' is complete, and follows through her intuition by adding—'Did it ever occur to you that you were all babying me, an old maid schoolteacher with nothing to do, writing a book about a young nephew she didn't really know from Adam or probably understand?' Such frankness is followed by her decision that she can now share with Boyd the news of Cliff's death, an account which releases in her the pent-up emotion of months, concluded by violent sobs of 'almost inhuman grief'. But a mutual rehabilitation is brought about as Boyd's realisation of the depth of his sister's suffering and need for comfort elicits new strength in him too. The same restorative powers are at work in the surrounding community, breaking up its inbred stasis, to effect other 'cures' and 'conversions'. Vernon Miller and Faye Laird dispense with the former secrecy of their alliance to publicise their forthcoming marriage—a move which defies the labels attached to them in the past, and continues the idea that strength in individuals stems from the ability to transcend the false pride that would deny their need for and dependence upon others. Even Minnie Clyde Hawke provides more 'news' (in another comic aside upon general trends) by her erratic and somewhat ostentatious progress towards the outstretched arms of Clara Himbaugh's 'Great Physician'.

As Alma and Boyd offer up their closely guarded secrets concerning Cliff's involvement with the two men next door, their misgivings are assuaged by the fact that they have been put into words at last. *Material* evidence is now recognised as misleading when divorced from the context that once gave it meaning—anything can be 'read' into it. In fact, the hoards of photographs and dollars signified only the process of secretion itself—both were memorials of feelings that were never expressed or understood. The old couple rely, instead, upon a deeper faith in Cliff to formulate the conviction that he was innocent of any wrong doing. That their nephew was not a thief is borne out by Vernon Miller's account, though the picture that does emerge is not without its pain. Alma's meeting with him has all the undercurrents of a dreamlike reunion with her nephew. He strays into her yard to observe the miracle of a butterfly so late in the year, resting on the snowball bush that marked the spot where he used to talk with Cliff. She studies the 'freshness and openness' of his face as if *in gratitude*, and makes the spontaneous gesture of inviting him inside. 'This is the first time I think I've ever been invited inside a Rainbow house,' he tells her. Alma, like Willard before her, opens her house, and her heart, to the 'nameless' orphan, to discover in him and to hear from him, what Cliff had been like:

> 'Cliff hated Rainbow,' Vernon began. 'He hated taking your and his uncle's charity. You were his Children's Home. He hated everything, I think. He hated being without parents and thinking he was unwanted. He hated for you to feel you had to love him. He never wanted to come back here or to hear from anybody. He told me, "If I had the money I would never be back." '

Alma is humbled and almost broken by Vernon's response to her plea for the truth, however painful that might be. But even knowing the extent of his unhappiness, her feelings for Cliff are undiminished. As she explains—'I see now how much he needed the little love anyone could give.' She carries the burden of her love in humility, without any trace of the old pride or the desire to see an idealised reflection of herself, and, apparently, without hope. This is not the final point in her search for knowledge, though, for Alma has still to apply all that she has learnt about the proud concealment of feelings in herself and in others, to Cliff himself.

71

The former irony of her determination to see her nephew's life in his 'omissions' takes on a new light, for he too is a victim of the prevalent recoil from investing the inner self in acts of communication. Whereas she had previously deciphered those 'omissions' in complacency, she must now approach them in sorrow and compassion and hope.

Although Vernon might faithfully have reproduced the 'truth' of Cliff's words, he also tells Alma that her nephew was too proud to admit that he needed love from anybody. By bringing into play his own resemblance to Cliff, he can recognise the pride that coloured those words and cut them off from other 'truths'. Both were 'adopted' by others, only to be torn inwardly by rivalling voices of doubt and belief as they scrutinised the language of those around them to discover whether they were objects of charity or were valued in themselves. In the case of Cliff, his aunt and uncle presented an enigmatic front since they habitually kept their true feelings at a distance from their words, and in consequence, their nephew 'adopted' the same habit out of self-protection. Vernon's picture of Cliff is very much that of his own past self, and in a sense, he now represents what his friend might have become if he had stayed and submitted to the painful uncertainties of love. In the past, Vernon, like Alma and Boyd, had hidden his love for Cliff in the hoard of photographs or the gift that had never been made explicit. But now, he too, can openly admit that love. Alma and Vernon can begin to make amends for the past by their present warmth and openness. They come to address one another by their Christian names, and Alma writes a dedication to that friendship on his newly plastered leg.

It is Mrs Barrington, however, who finally helps her to come to terms with her doubt and to understand her nephew's involvement in the generalised retreat from the expression of need. Their conversation is prefaced by reminders of the relentless flux of time— to use Alma's words—'things changed imperceptibly for a while, then unrecognizably'. The failings of health and old age are echoed in the dereliction of treasured symbols and illusions; 'Memorial Day' has come once more, but a physical mishap precipitates the process of decay at work in the fabric to reduce the flag, 'Old Glory', to a mass of shreds; the ferocious winter gales have razed the precious landmarks in Mrs Barrington's gardens, and she, at last, is immobilised. Nonetheless, the novel's ultimate voice is one of affirmation—the outer tokens of celebration, the flags and the monumental gardens, make way for a more wistful appreciation of life's memorable qualities, its pains and rewards. From out of the surrounding decline comes the burgeoning of a new intimacy as, for the first time, the two women have a 'real talk'. Mrs Barrington, after a lifetime of concealing the truth about herself, reveals the pain of her loveless marriage and the strategies she employed to dissimulate that void. Alma's frankness is even readier, for whereas the monarch had prepared herself to approach her friend's troubles 'step by step in gradual and easy descent', she finds her volunteering information in advance of such sophistries. Yet she refutes Alma's avowal that she was never loved, insisting that Vernon might have told the 'truth' as he heard it, but—'it wasn't the truth as your nephew felt it', and countering the fact that he had wanted to run away, by asking— 'Who doesn't want to run away from those they love, and at his age?' Alma opens herself to the healing faith, to the calming authority of one who has known similar sorrow and can 'read' the 'omissions' of others in the dazzling light of her own, and so she arrives at the 'Threshold of Assent' as this last chapter is so aptly entitled with its further hint of her readiness for the final peace of that other 'Great Physician'—death.

At the very end, she and Boyd sit together in the darkness, composing, by their spontaneous upsurges of 'real talk', a far more meaningful 'memorial' to their nephew than the showing of flags, the hoarding of souvenirs or the projection of biographies. They testify to the recovery of the faculty that had been missing from their lives by sharing and formulating their inner thoughts and feelings, at peace in one another's company. Boyd's strong voice issues out of that darkness to assure her that—'Cliff knew we cared, Alma . . . that made him care too, at last, though he maybe never said it, and he didn't have the gift, you and I know, to write it.' Alma, in turn, shows how much she now values that 'gift', and her pain is eased by her ability to say— 'I'm so glad you've been here, Boyd. It would be pretty all-alone by myself.' Words are reinfused with their deepest human functions, a rare phenomenon amongst the inhabitants of Purdy's dark world.

3

Cabot Wright Begins and *Eustace Chisholm and the Works*

Purdy's next two novels, *Cabot Wright Begins* (1964) and *Eustace Chisholm and the Works* (1967), form a new stage in that underlying biography of the possibilities and constrictions of selfhood in the different phases of existence. The relationship of the child or adolescent to parental figures which was a major preoccupation of the earlier fiction is now succeeded by a fuller vision of the adult world of sexual love in which the quest for identity must be pursued. In keeping with this broadening perspective, there is a more direct engagement with contemporary society. One aim would seem to be that of constructing 'biographical' portraits of two distinct periods in recent American history. The central characters are eminently representative individuals; Cabot's life has all the makings of a 'success story' that embodies the ideals of post-war consumer society; Eustace is the archetypal victim of the Depression years. But if a biography is to be considered a 'real-life' story, then the fact that both characters are the medium of historical forces becomes increasingly ironic. The author can only suggest the failure of those two epochs to make room for the 'real' ingredients of life.

Cabot Wright Begins dramatises the exclusion of such qualities in a complex manner. It depicts the attempts of various writer figures to compile the definitive life-history of one of their contemporaries, a phenomenal rapist. Unfortunately, despite his actual collaboration in the venture, their human subject performs endless disappearing tricks, evaporating from the combined endeavour to commit the truth about him to paper. The 'real' Cabot Wright's ostentatious escape from his own biography might be construed as a comic endorsement of D. H. Lawrence's notion that the biggest difficulty in fiction was to find a means of transporting the living essence of a character into the novel without its dying in the process. Thus Purdy might seem to have the twofold intention of parodying aspects of 'popular' and 'highbrow' fiction; the sexual prurience of the one genre being mischievously crossed with the other's delight in making a novel's genesis its essential subject and dwelling learnedly upon the nature of the perceptual processes. Indeed, several critics have felt obliged to qualify their appreciation of the author's talents on the grounds that he appears to be mocking his own activities as a novelist. Such reservations arise when Purdy's writer figures are interpreted as ironic reflectors of some entrenched aesthetic pessimism on his part, as pawns in a discourse upon the futility of art's pretensions to engage with reality.

But this seems an unnecessary trivialisation of his formal subtleties. Purdy's novel is not written from the point of view of some misanthropic philosopher with an array of literary axes to grind, but from that of someone whose faith in the redeeming qualities of language and whose affection for the homely idioms of native speech is affronted by the perverse chorus of their manipulation for commercial ends and by the devitalised cultural homogeneity that results. The type of literature he attacks is seen as a microcosm of the society it panders to. The underlying ethos of which these aspirant writers are the agents is the primary target for satire. The elements of literary parody translate themselves on to another level to compose what might well be described as an ontological detective story, addressing itself to the disappearance of man's innermost being or soul. Lawrence's formulation of a perennial artistic problem is more applicable in the sense that Purdy depicts society as a mammoth 'potboiler'. That individual 'living essence' expires beneath the constrictions of social forces operating like the mechanics of novelistic form in anarchic divorce from their traditional engagement with spiritual values.

Such reductions are both simulated and exposed in the form of *Cabot Wright Begins*. The correspondences that are progressively uncovered between apparently disparate phenomena converge in the comic paradox of Cabot's double billing as Beauty and the Beast. The exemplary business man with classic features is simultaneously a demonic rapist—*but* the first of these roles comes to usurp the title of monstrous violator of civilised values, whilst the second appropriates the laurels of philanthropic instructor in the norms of behaviour! His investigators are hoist with their own petard as the 'meaning' of those rapes becomes apparent—to the reader, at least. Their attempt to inject a topicality into his story overreaches itself when the rapist proves to be indistinguishable from a society that assaults and anaesthetises inner being. Life in such an environment cannot begin to acquire a spiritual dimension, to form a consistent 'narrative'. Past and future are contained within an endless present. In accordance with its title, the novel veritably bristles with 'beginnings'. Every episode teases us with the notion of progress, with 'cures' and fresh starts, with an array of distinctive characters—but the only movements are those of a collapse into an underlying sameness, of identities that dissolve into the blankness of a wall. Indeed, that wall is the central and pervasive image. It is the mirror of a world where life's flux and variety have been reduced to an 'Indelible Smudge', as the luck-less Bernie Gladhart's novel about Cabot Wright is finally entitled. But the inscription on this wall is as plain as its Old Testament antecedent, or that other more native wall that imaged the fixity of death-in-life for Bartleby, the scrivener, of Melville's short story.

We are first alerted to these multiplying correspondences that infiltrate the text like the bacillus of the 'American disease' it describes, by the fact that Purdy begins *his* novel with a lengthy portrait of the characters who are inspired to write Cabot's story. Their version of his career is held back until the seventh chapter. In retrospect, this opening section could be seen to have told us all there is to know about our hero. His literary genesis forms a prophetic anticipation of the forces that are subsequently seen to have shaped his 'life'. It gives us our first vision of *the writing on the wall*.

The great novel that is supposed to haunt the literary (and commercial) imagination with the potency of the American dream itself, is launched when Bernie Gladhart, a second-hand car sales-man, is propelled towards the dizzy heights of bestsellerdom by the fierce energies of his wife . . .

77

Carrie, a semi-retired miniature painter, believed confidently that her husband Bernie had, as she always put it, a 'great book inside of him', if only for once he could start out with the right subject: his other books, unpublished, were about himself and had been perhaps too personal to have wide appeal. Not only was Carrie certain that Bernie would write a great book, she was also convinced that it would reach the big public. Great books, if long enough and full of topical description and contemporary comment, were now coming into even wider public favour.

The elements of parody here are fairly obvious: the exploits of a notorious rapist are to be framed by a pseudo-scientific investigation in the new vogue for authenticity and the Ishmaelite Bernie is packed off in quest of New York's White Whale with the injunction to 'write the truth like fiction' ringing in his ears. More interesting is the way Purdy takes up the challenge that 'topical description' and 'contemporary comment' are the hallmarks of the new novel. Just as Bernie is required to 'dig' into Cabot's impeccable past, these opening chapters unearth the hero's literary ancestry in a way that sardonically matches the 'topicality' of that promised 'inside story'.

His genealogy is charted in imagery which suggests that sexuality has dwindled to a meretricious form of literary creation, and vice versa. His literary 'mother' runs her marriage on the same lines as the popular novel that wraps its sensational subject in a glossy package. Carrie's enormous sexual appetite is secured by the church-like edifice of 'faith' she builds up around her husband. Rooms and buildings are always crucial symbols in Purdy's work. Bernie is promoted from mere 'roomer' to the 'wedding-bower' perched in heavenly isolation at the top of the house. Carrie's pet phrases are tokens of the fixity she introduces into life; transients are drawn by the signs she hangs outside the house, she holds out the illusion of a 'home'. But the 'wedding-bower' suggests a staged *setting*, a place where everything is always beginning. Indeed, the sanctuary where the inner self would seem most likely to be 'penetrated' turns out to be the domain of blankness. Bernie's imprisonment within a 'permanent erection', however church-like its exterior, anticipates Cabot's plight:

> Every night in Chicago at 9.15 p.m., Bernie mounted the winding staircase, in his dressing robe, to Carrie's huge bedroom at the top

of the landing, and for fifteen interminable minutes, man and wife thrashed vigorously together among the bedclothes. Roomers who had returned early heard Carrie, at the end of the quarter of the hour, cry out, 'I'm going! Dying! I'm going, you hear?' Bernie, battling to keep his virile member belligerent, fought out the quarter hour, until his wife's cries signalled success; then he retired from the fray, keeping what he had bottled up, as it were, for the exigencies of the next night.

The images of a death-like motion and the bottling up of life's fluids make a wry comment on that great book Bernie was to release from inside, if only he began with the right subject.

The marriage that fails so singularly to connect is framed by an account of the Gladharts' 'society'. The Saturday evening parties held one week at their house and the next at the Bickles, are as ritualistic as that nightly performance in the 'wedding-bower'. Although more or less the same people attend each gathering, discussion is the rule at the Bickles and perfunctory sexual encounters at the Gladharts. This polarisation of words and feeling, that causes each to be negated, takes place throughout the novel. It is comically reiterated in both marital relationships; we are told that Zoe Bickle adamantly attributes the success of her marriage to Curt's perpetual failure as a writer, whilst Carrie is convinced hers will fail unless Bernie achieves literary fame. The pattern is completed when Curt is agreed to have all the training and verbal skills required of a writer, but to be totally lacking in the life-experience and feeling, which are all Bernie possesses.

Cabot's literary life springs from these polarities. He is a hybrid of the two parties, of words wrenched from context and of feelings made phantasmagoric by their divorce from communicable forms. Thus the seeds sown by a newspaper clipping of the 'right' subject's availability and by casual remarks snatched from their intended sarcasm at one of the discussion evenings, fall on fertile ground in the perfunctory genre of Carrie's sexual encounters. Cabot is born of her inner vacuum and delivered by Zoe's suggestion that Bernie's dispatch is the 'writing on the wall' of her unacknowledged desire to make room for the next Mr Right. The point is pushed home when Carrie manages to resemble nothing more than a frame that had lost its picture. There is little wonder, then, that Bernie attributes his plight to his wife's approaching 'menopause'; he decides, confusedly, that 'Cabot Wright seemed to be a change-of-life baby, so far as she was concerned.' His *translation* to Brooklyn stems, appropriately, from her appetite for *novelty*. A fresh chapter is added to the 'potboiler' of that existence when another roomer is promoted to the office of stopping the gaps. Carrie's abrupt transition from one extreme to another is typical of many characters in the novel: few show any coherence of outer and inner self. The wilful belief in Bernie's literary future, needed to frame her sexual appetite and to inject some 'topicality' into her marriage, undergoes a complete reversal . . .

> Those phone calls told her, for on the telephone one finally hears the real voice isolated from the flesh that contains it. What she heard coming from Brooklyn was only a mewling infant missing its milk. It had been a kind of drug to believe the impossible, to believe in Bernie, but suddenly her belief was dead.

But her reversal is caused to fall back on her. The regression to death, to the perpetual beginning, underlies each episode: Bernie is brought back to zero when he finds himself on the receiving end of telephonic mewling sounds emanating from Chicago. The soundtrack that accompanies the arrival of a little 'colour' into the pallor of the vacant 'wedding-bower' makes him feel like a man who tuned into the radio only to hear the announcement of his own death. Carrie is so engrossed in the clasps of her lascivious Moor that she forgets to replace the receiver after one of the communications intended to top up her husband's inspiration. In such a travesty of the sexual relation life's real creative potential is effaced. Adults reduce themselves to the stature of children and the only offspring of such a marriage of fictions is the 'change-of-life baby', a substitute for the 'real thing'. The great book that was locked inside can only issue forth with the noise of the still-born.

Bernie's substitution for the 'real thing' in terms of his marriage, turns out to make him peculiarly equipped to be the author of Cabot's biography. The initial absurdity of his credentials as second-hand car salesman is reversed when we appreciate the family likeness of literary 'father' and 'son'. Though under orders to 'write the truth like fiction', Bernie cannot locate his 'main character' and has to assemble a manuscript at second-hand from old newspapers and magazines. But this is a repeat of his own life story and so, unwittingly, he *does* write the truth like fiction. Furthermore, since 'fiction' or substitutions for the 'real thing' are at the root of his common ancestry with Cabot, the biography he compiles contains the 'truth' about him too.

These correspondences are projected with meticulous irony. The notion of an 'inside story', for example, is elaborated in terms of rooms and buildings once more. In Brooklyn Bernie is homesick, lost in the city's anonymity, and plagued by his old feeling of being in front of a closed door. In common with his fictional progeny, he too is an ex-criminal, though neither could be said to have turned to crime with customary motivations. Bernie broke into houses in a confused hope of finding himself on the 'inside', at home with the occupants. But the only interiors he had ever really known were those that confirmed his lack of a self-determined identity— the orphanage, and later the reformatory. Even the 'break-ins' that took place in Carrie's 'wedding-bower' were part of this pattern. Thus it is right that he should discover his elusive 'main character' in residence within his own domain. Their crumbling tenement serves as a microcosm of New York and of a society given over to one-way communications. See-River Manor is likened to a huge listening booth; it affords neither privacy nor a sense of community; it hums with sound, but none of it is grounded in genuine contact between individuals. The circumstances of his literary break-through are full of prophetic irony. He investigates an unintelligible stream of sound that percolates through the floor of the tiny closet where he kept his clothes. A loose board is removed to disclose an empty shaft affording an insight into the room immediately below. The 'forlorn yellowed habitation', apparently empty but for some dreary looking books, suggests a little world of dead words that mirrors Bernie's only 'home'. On another occasion he espies someone, 'as we catch a glimpse unexpectedly of our own worried face in a store window and do not immediately recognise who is staring back at us'. The encounter of biographer and raw materials leads only to a stunned silence. Cabot can only shout up an absent-minded warning for his voyeur *not to begin*. There isn't much chance of this, though. The meeting images the circularity of Bernie's life; he is brought face to face with his own non-self and is back at the point of committing a 'break-in'—to find nobody at home.

81

Each semblance of progress is overtaken by an emanation from the void as the excesses of the imagination die in their own too much. Bernie's past catches up with him endlessly to erase the fictions he constructs around his 'main character'. That past takes shape through the offices of Zoe Bickle, whom he comes to think of quite rightly as the force which spun his destiny. Accordingly, his precious manuscript is wrenched from his possession by Princeton Keith, Zoe's childhood sweetheart and editor of a giant publishing corporation. Zoe herself arrives soon afterwards to take over the project altogether. Hired at a fabulous fee, she is to supply the brains and the English language to expunge Bernie's 'mentality' from the present draft. The underlying sameness of Cabot and Bernie is thus anticipated when the latter is stripped of his last semblance of self-expression to be re-written in another's idiom. He remains the 'author' of an existence in name only.

Mrs Bickle is the prime example of language's detachment from the inner self. Carrie once accused her of working at never saying or showing what she felt, thought, or was. On another occasion Cabot asks, 'If somebody told you the story of your own life, Mrs Bickle, in New York newspaper English, wouldn't you disremember yourself too?' But this is precisely what has happened to her; she has buried all feelings in marriage to just such a chunk of newspaper English, she lives by hard little editing jobs, by 'fixing' things. As the purveyor of words that cloak rather than elucidate meaning, she is the ideal servant of the publishing fraternity when it interests itself only in following the dictates of commerce. But if life's mobility is reduced to a set of clichés, Cabot is caused to redirect these towards their source with sardonic accuracy. For example, the cliché takes on a comic life of its own when Bernie's stalemate is duplicated in a second literary (and literal) break-through that runs up against a blank wall. Whilst deliberating on the etiquette of securing an entrée to the rapist's domicile, Zoe 'drops in' unceremoniously through a glass skylight during the panic of an imagined fire alert. The abrupt fall from one level to another suggests a descent into the inner compartments of her own psyche. Her habitual *self-composure* is rudely shattered as she plummets into the zone of emotional aridity created by her own professional detachment and policy of disinterest. The episode

82

gives a comic rendering of the vacancy of self that lies under *assignment*.

Respectable American matrons and convicted rapists might seem necessarily limited to forced connections, yet there is much irony as the two figures become inseparably entwined in the portrait of anaesthesia and spiritual emptiness this narrative compiles. Cabot presents Zoe with the offspring of her detachment—he is such an amalgam of disparate images, accents even, that there is no cohesion or continuity in the persona he projects. Her unconventional arrival is greeted with nonchalance *and* giggles. She is dazed by her efforts to reconcile the bland exterior of Mr Right, society's dream boy, 'the mythical clean cut American youth out of Coca-Cola ads, church socials, picnics along the lake . . .' with the knowledge that he is also the veteran of an incredible career of rape upon those clichéd ideals. The notion of nobody (and everybody!) being at home in his consciousness is reiterated in the description of his room. For instance, he makes a point of drawing Zoe's attention to the peculiarities of his wallpaper and explains how the stereotyped and layered patterns gradually wear down to the bare plaster underneath. Here, as elsewhere, Cabot becomes the spokesman of the underlying emptiness of contemporary life, as if he drew a paradoxical sense of identity from anonymity itself. He seems proud of the fact that at least his impersonal room with its crumbling decorations is an authentic reproduction of his own period, unlike the dream-palace his adopted parents had concocted. Mrs Bickle is addressed as though she *were* the wallpaper—with an odd justice since she is the fabricator of such commercial patterns in the word industry. The image of fictions recreating and reverting to the blank they were meant to cover up unites Cabot and Mrs Bickle, causing them both to merge back into that wall.

The querulous, half-stifled voice in Zoe that says there is *no story* here, is not allowed to interfere with her assemblage of patterns once her assignment jerks back into motion and away from its dead end after Cabot offers himself as collaborator. But the separation of her consciousness into two parts causes each to negate the other: professional disinterest enables her to work at Bernie's manuscript, whilst that suppressed interest nags and reminds her that fiction is being compounded with fiction since the 'meaning' of those rapes is as elusive as ever. To understand Cabot would be to 'coax' the truth out of herself too. Yet this combination of qualities in Zoe provides Cabot with an opportunity of reversing the one-way communications that have poured into him from all channels in his society. Her latent curiosity suggests a patience her predecessors lacked, whereas her passive detachment will hold her incomprehension in abeyance, thus allowing him to see his story 'written out straight'. He thinks of her as the ideal 'ear' and 'tongue' to cure him of his own unreality so that he might then go on to become somebody else. There is a comic appropriateness in having a *ghost writer* to exorcise and dispossess him of his phantasmagoric self.

It is hardly surprising, then, that the extracts from that biography arrive with a decided air of the déjà vu. Novelised by Bernie from a hotch-potch of materials, it has been revised by Zoe with the assistance of equally second-hand sources in Cabot himself. As 'proof-reader' he can only verify what the extracts make abundantly clear—that he is a stranger to the story itself. The inconsistencies of earlier versions that Zoe inwardly despairs of ever sorting out, especially as Cabot delights in pointing out the more obvious blunders, re-arrange themselves with a comic logic in Purdy's encompassing novel. His prologue to their text has provided us with the key with which to unravel its mirror-writing. The 'main character's' loss, brought about by his authors' pretentions to objectivity, turns out to incorporate their story too. The counterfeiting of the book corresponds exactly to the societal forces that had fabricated Cabot's identities in the first place. A fiction mirrors his *life as fiction*, to instill a 'verisimilitude' that is more topical than anything Carrie could have dreamed up.

The paradoxical 'meaning' of those rapes slowly incriminates the whole of the surrounding society. Far from being some obnoxious freak of humanity, Cabot emerges as normalcy writ large. Any suggestion that he stands beyond the pale of 'civilisation' is ironically undermined, until by the end of the story we are more ready to capitulate to him as some saintly apostle! Whereas rape customarily denotes an anarchic, barbarous act, Cabot's assaults are as perfunctory as those trysts in Carrie's 'wedding-bower'. For example:

A window would be shattered.

'It's time, Mrs Van Buren,' Cabot would say, stepping into a neat parlour and unbuttoning his fly. 'I haven't but a moment.'

'I know,' Mrs Van Buren would answer stoically.

'Then remove your clothes, sweetheart. You can leave on the light.'

There is an absurd contrast between the lascivious imaginings of his would-be publishers ('have him jab them in every paragraph') and the matter-of-fact execution of the act. The *prosaic* approach of the 'rapist' is reciprocated by that of his 'victim'. We learn that they would telephone the police not so much to register a complaint as to share the experience. With Cabot, even rape is a substitute for the 'real thing'.

If the essential Cabot is not to be found in his rapes, neither is there much trace of him in the outward events of his life. But the disappearance is itself significant. The twin forces that bring about his literary genesis have their counterpart in the dual careers he pursues. Just as Carrie is delivered of a 'change-of-life baby', so Cabot's worldly parents procure themselves a 'supposititious' child to be moulded in their image. They supply him with a societal identity without consulting his inner needs; his adjustment to the 'handwriting on the wall', as they like to call it, necessitates a wife and an apartment each as fashionable and as expensive as the other, and a position on Wall Street itself. Any sense of his own reality predictably withers beneath this translation. His only token of rebellion is to walk to work across the Brooklyn Bridge, though we notice the Statue of Liberty is almost always obscured in the mist. He develops a feeling of total fatigue which this one resistance to the 'right' impression cannot keep at bay for long and so his other 'beginning' is brought on by a visit to a strange doctor, supposedly an expert in dealing with the new 'tired feeling'. The 'cure' for what is instantly diagnosed as 'American disease' is effected by draping him over a large hook and inciting him to 'let go' . . .

> Struggling on the immense mattress-padded hook which had come out of the wall, Cabot felt very much like a fish—caught but not pulled in. The blood rushed violently to his head. His shorts, which he had laundered many times, snapped, and fell down about his legs. Visions of gauchos riding on the pampas came to him, to-

gether with memories of bull-fights he had seen on TV. His forehead was swimming with sweat, he felt his intestines give, spittle flowed freely from his mouth, and his navel suddenly contracting violently seemed to explode and vanish, as will the top crust of a pie in the oven when the proper slits have not been made in it. Cabot felt he was saying *adios* from a boat rapidly advancing from the shore on which stood his adopted father and mother in their Florida clothes, and his recent bride, Mrs Cabot Wright Junior in her Vogue pattern dress.

The imagery is suggestive: Cabot is only offered an illusion of freedom, he is still a fish that is hooked, if not yet pulled in. If he is *fixed* by his position on Wall Street, this second career is equally constricting. After all, a *permanent erection*, procured mysteriously by a hook on another wall, is hardly an antidote to the loss of reality engendered by the rigidity of social roles. It implies that if, on the one hand, the individual is devoured by the impersonal institutions of a commercial world, then identity is equally threatened by the secret gurus who effect some regression to a mere bodily existence, treating a spiritual malaise as though it were a malfunctioning of the libido. The image of Cabot setting out on a voyage of discovery is just as treacherous. Far from escaping America, he is to act out its underlying history. It is worth recalling the fate of his namesake, the English seaman, Cabot, who vanished during his explorations of America and whose son was the prophet of that famous and disastrous chimera, the north-west passage—a dead end.

These early suggestions that Cabot's 'cure' will be as dehumanising as his 'disease' are borne out when we learn more about the doctor in question. Bigelow-Martin undergoes his own transformation; he assumes a variety of names, invariably forgetting those of his clients; his activities have given rise to as many contradictory accounts of his origins as there are audiences to be fleeced; some customers are incited to 'flow', others are urged into the straitjackets of conformity. He would seem to be the shaping spirit of this society, its secret artist, subversive of individual values only. He operates to remove all sense of inner direction, re-adjusting those whose sense of dissatisfaction is a potential threat to the prevailing ethos. The opiate of mindless sexual gratification and that of a comatose relaxation is released in those with a loss of conviction in their societal roles. Elsewhere, in the Marriage-or-Death Clinic, individual energies and preferences are clamped down by an equally mindless subservience to the God of hetero-sexuality. Bigelow-Martin is another of Cabot's many 'fathers'—but the filial obedience he induces in this case is so total that it quite defeats its objective.

Purdy's novel is built up around such strange reversals. There are many such oppositions and paired qualities in the course of the narrative: interest/disinterest, right/wrong, cure/disease, inside/outside, erection/flow, blank wall/pattern, to name but a few. It is as if some peculiar law of compensation were in being, whereby the fixity of any one quality engendered its antithesis to bring about its own negation. What seem to be absolute polarities crumble into sameness. For example, we are presented with the catalogue of myths the various media weave around the demon in their midst; each ethnic group endows him with the features of their antagonists until these stereotypes blur into a polyglot identity and what started out by being blatantly 'wrong' turns into just the 'right' image of Cabot's anonymity.

The Wright marriage is fractured in this way. Instead of contain-ing the newly released energies which were to have inured the hero to his life, it disintegrates under the completeness of his 'cure'. Man and wife gravitate to opposing extremes: Cabot's purely instinctual 'manhood' is as much a travesty of human possibilities as the ideals of femininity his wife, Cynthia, culls from her fashion magazines. She recedes further and further from the bodily realities he has rediscovered until pregnancy becomes synonymous with death. 'Sexual commerce' is warded off in the name of 'civilisation', she barricades herself in the bedroom and regresses to the mentality of a little girl. She breaks down in her own 'too much', mouthing garbled versions of radio announce-ments and finally 'letting go' in the local supermarket. Though she had intended to get 'food' for Cabot, she ends up smashing a whole range of items into a sticky mess—another version of that collapse into an 'Indelible (if not inedible) Smudge'.

Cabot, meanwhile, journeys in another direction to become an extended 'listening' device, absorbing and regurgitating indiscrim-inately whatever banality flows into his ear. At another level, he develops an 'interest'—in tropical plants and their methods of propagation! But the books he studies in the local library sow their own subliminal seeds in his mind, he reads, for example . . . 'Sometimes when a plant is grown in a foreign country artificial pollination must be resorted to . . .' Always obedient to the 'message', this is what would seem to awaken Cabot to his new vocation. The library concentrates the surrounding society's soporific effect upon him, as if it constituted that 'foreign country' hostile to the transmission of life where artificial measures had to be adopted in order to ensure the survival of the species. Thus his inaugural rape takes place after he has persuaded a young woman to join him for a breath of fresh air. She nods agreement in 'her eviscerated debrained sweatered grace' as though she were one of Cynthia's blueprints. They step through a hole in a wall into an adjacent room which is dark and empty. It is as if they stepped straight from a Bickles' party into one of the Gladharts'. Together they act out the secret life of their society where sexuality and verbal communication have been hived off into separate compartments. Whilst his actress companion had been researching a new part, Cabot has been *remembered* in an older one. But sex is symbolically on a par with other bodily functions; saliva and sweat are excreted as mechanically as semen. The Old Testament idiom of 'knowing' another person, with its suggestion that intercourse involves the metaphysical roots of being, is comically absent. We are back to the hook and the wall. Cabot utters the enigmatic words 'Get deadly' as a benediction upon his new career, suggesting that in a world where pregnancy is synonymous with death, his philanthropic pollinations must bring about the demise of the fictions preferred by such as his wife.

The rapes all fall into this pattern, the predictability of Cabot's behaviour being matched by the beneficiaries of his new gospel. He provides them all with a *beginning* by injecting his sharp reminder that their lives had lost all meaning. None of them make more than a token resistance, faithful children of the age of advertising, they are open to each and every 'message'. The origin of life is pumped into them as if to insist that the only fresh start possible would be one based on an awakening to their own anaesthesia.

The 'major' biographical rapes develop this notion in detail, and it is worth looking at one of the funniest—the 'conversion' of Gilda, the wife of Cabot's employer. She had been primed to 'cure' him of his strange lapses from 'civilised' behaviour at work. These had been attributed somewhat over hastily to the twin catastrophes that had overtaken him: Cynthia's relegation to the 'nuthatch' and his parents' abrupt deaths in the revolutionary Carribean. In fact neither event had done more than to provoke the odd giggle in him in recognition of the absurdity of life in general. Like her husband, Gilda delivers set speeches. Language goes on mechanically even though its informing spirit is dead. Though neither of them are really listening, the supposedly funereal guest is treated to her popular lecture on how, in the current of the present, she had got rid of her European servants (though they were loves) and had engaged coloured personnel in the hope of being brought into closer touch with the realities of the present. But Cabot is to confront her with those realities in an earlier version of the lesson he imparts to Zoe Bickle with regard to the wallpaper and the wall. As her name suggests, Gilda glosses over the vacuity of her existence. Employment is traded for the gratification of her jaded appetite in the 'sexual commerce' she practices with her servant. Cabot's impassivity in the face of her stilted and ceremonious circumlocutions causes them to crumble in their own banality. They are both refreshed by a good giggle. The truth of her situation is brought home more tellingly when her guest steps in with the 'dessert' Brady was wont to furnish. But Gilda, in the terminal stages of 'American disease', is too far gone to be sure that either man had 'touched' her. Nonetheless, her experience enlightens her sufficiently to be able to round on her husband and accuse him of having brought even more vacuum than money into her existence. She goes on to search feebly for the right version . . . 'in order to remain, as she said, a functioning plant (she had given up her attempt of a few years ago to be a functioning animal)'.

If we look at one of the 'minor' rapes, the same pattern repeats itself, endorsing the notion that Cabot is America in action. He explains to Zoe how the lady in question, Bertha McIntosh, was hoist on to his bannister in the middle of her mission as municipal agent and forced to recognise that everybody in America got 'screwed'. The act spells out her life-long submission to 'rape', she had surrendered up her individual self to become the passive agent of a manipulative society. Brought to feel the sickening pain of that position, she can formulate that past as one where a monster crouched over her, quelling the pleasure of nausea even, such a conformist had she been. But these philanthropic seeds fall on barren ground and her 'beginning' is as abortive as all the others. We learn of the new life that plastered over the momentary recognition of emptiness; suburbia and a sterile marriage exchange one 'wallpaper' for another and she ends her days in devotion to 'the interesting recent hobbies of collecting butterfly nets and early post-Victorian paperweights'.

Cabot's contemporaneity is only fully appreciated in the context of his relations with his employer, Mr Warburton. His empire, built up according to the traditional ethic of devotion to work, recapitulates the nation's history. He rails against the dissipation of those founding energies in the present generation in the daily lectures intended to groom Cabot for the top. 'Listening' was one of his principal duties, here, as in the larger world. But the attempts to mould Cabot in his own image are somewhat ironic since the youthful rapist is already Warburton's creation in a deeper sense. The patriarch is bewildered by the cuckoo-like 'change-of-life baby' the old American dream has unwittingly fostered. His outrage is most vehement in the 'Sermons' he secretly compiles. For instance:

> America, which began as a society of men with plans, confidence, and good blood in its veins . . . has ended in shambles of scrofulous obscenity and barking half-breeds in which nothing worth selling or connecting is hawked, barked and exposed in its inadequate meretricious shine to a nation of uninterested buyers. Young and old have suffered and are suffering a series of consumer haemorrhages from a non-attendant civilisation that has only noise, confusion, pumped-up virility and pornography.

But the deadliness he decries is the inevitable outcome of his own single-minded pursuit of material goals. His one-way communications to Cabot are as neglectful of the individual self as those moronic messages that drool from all the outlets of the mass media. The 'wild oats' he boasts of having sown in his youth have come to fruition.

The ironic convergence of what appear to be two completely un-

connected 'careers' forms the central motif in the narrative. Warburton echoes Bigelow-Martin's and society's recipe for the fatigue
they have collectively introduced: sex is the universal placebo and
Cabot is ordered to give up sleep for the good of the nation, to go
away and 'explode'. But that 'explosion' backfires upon its authors.
The fictions Warburton spins around the disaffection of his junior
executive come into direct collision with the 'inside story'. Gilda's
ailing memory is restored when Cabot obligingly rapes the friend,
Zenda Stuyvesant, who was to 'size up' his offensive potential. The
old man is the only one who acknowledges his complicity in siring
an absurd world, an embittered acceptance which is expressed in
the revisions he carries out to the documentation of his life. The
'Sermons' spring from his 'buried self', to contrast sharply with
Zoe Bickle's inability to formulate the self that is interred within
her assignment. Those 'Sermons' gush similarly from the heart of
Purdy's novel, suggesting the ferment of revulsion that at times
forces an exit through the comic indirections of its surface layers.
The tone of voice projected through Warburton is that of the
omniscient author himself. In Chapter 18, for example, Purdy
takes over the narrative that has disintegrated under Zoe's pen to
recapitulate Cabot's 'problem':

> Dr Bigelow-Martin had taken away all his attention except in his
> erectile tissue, and the police hoses and night-sticks had removed
> his attention there. But was this not the problem of the whole
> USA? Under the different Generals, poker-players, country squires,
> haberdashers, grandsons of whiskey-barons for President, and while
> America is fucking the rest of the world or putting a yellow island
> down the incinerator in the name of freedom, wearing Jehovah's
> whiskers and the tiara of the Queen of Heaven, the fact remains
> that the American people at home, *chez eux*, to quote Princeton
> Keith, outside of the aged and aging who are crying their heads
> off for free doctors and rectal TV, the rest of the USA citizenry,
> as a noted magazine calls them, from Maine's retired millionaires
> to the shores of the gilded Yukon, the American people are all head-
> wise, if not psychic-wise anaesthetic.

Like Warburton, the author 'lets go' a flood of diatribes, just as
Cabot puts his 'victims' up against the wall to puncture the fictions
they inhabit.

But if Cabot and his employer are involved in a process of

mutual destruction, they also help one another to a partial re-habilitation. Whereas the whole cast of characters caught up in Cabot's 'life as fiction' remain regally unamused by the image of themselves he reflects, Warburton releases the capacity to laugh at himself and at his creation. His ultimate revision is that of his last will and testament. Cabot is recognised as his only heir, his 'adopted son' in fact. The bitter edge to his laughter is borne out by his subsequent suicide, underlining the paradox upon which the whole novel is based—that the seeds of renewal in this world are necessarily those of destruction. The convergence of the two 'careers' is embodied in Gilda's comment that Cabot has ascended from *General Partner* to *God* in her husband's empire. Anaesthesia rules! The rapaciousness of business America has engendered its only Messiah—the assault by the knowledge of its own emptiness. The empire that had been held together by irritability, greed, tension and an underlying misanthropy is pro-phetically dispersed by the non-self it has brought into being. Life's constriction into one mould has caused the vessel to burst; Cabot discharges that bottled-up 'living essence' in every direc-tion, just as he pours the fortune he inherits back into the void it covered up—that army of the homeless written out of the govern-ment's statistical version of Moneycup America.

The collapse of that empire from within is duplicated by that of the literary enterprise that mushroomed into being around Cabot. The book that was fathered by Princeton Keith's greed is wiped out by a more pugnacious brand in Al Guggelhaupt, 'Goethe' of publishers. The end product is tasted and found wanting by almost as many critics as it had had authors. 'Indelible Smudge' is declared unfit for human consumption (though the message of its title is unwittingly reproduced when the book itself is obliterated beneath the motley of prescriptions directed at it). The market forces that had ordained its production in the first place have mis-calculated its topicality, by at least two years! It contradicts the last minute predictions of all the literary astrologers: rape is *passé* in the new age of 'the black faggot and fellatio'.

By the end of the narrative, the characters involved in the aborted biography are all dispersed, in every sense. They are back to where they were in the beginning, only more so! The 'news' of their various fates is predictably stale. Princeton Keith finally realises he is like the hollow inside a statue. Zoe Bickle retreats behind the wall of her marriage. For a while, Cabot's letters remind her of her 'main character's' escape, but any 'interest' in that phenomenon is carefully shuttered behind the habitual mask of cynicism. She declares to her husband that she won't be a writer in a time and place like the present—another fact we have been well aware of all along. Carrie's news bulletin is old history too: 'Mama's well is dry', is the message that greets the prodigal, that is, as far as her 'newly' contracted ailment, 'television glint', will allow her to concentrate on his return. And Bernie, superfluous as ever, can only rediscover his vocation as second-hand car salesman.

Thus the self-defeating nature of what appeared to promise 'progress' is asserted everywhere in the novel. Its cannibalism of form offers itself as a revised version of the national history, calling into question the supposed advancement and enrichments of the post-war consumer paradise. The national self that is depicted as having been 'stuffed' with fictions (the 'bloat' recommended as literature's latest ingredient by one of Guggelhaupt's advisers is already incorporated with a vengeance) is deflated by Purdy's determined counter-assault. He administers an 'emetic' in comic form. As for Cabot, the deadly images of his biographers' dessication and dispersal are juxtaposed with what would seem to be that long awaited 'beginning'. Although he scarcely rises phoenix-like from their ashes, he has inherited Warburton's discovery of laughter as a regenerative force. Those 'Sermons' had finally provided him with the 'inside story' on his parentage and Zoe Bickle furnished the medium through which to discharge and purge himself of all the fictions he had imbibed. He makes the first tentative steps towards the discovery of an inner identity that is in contact with the outer world when he graduates from giggles to a genuine laugh. The allusions to his future suggest the consolidation of this inner direction—the letters to Zoe, which already have the ring of Warburton's embittered proselytising, imply a flight which is also a form of confrontation. He declares that he is becoming a 'professional laugher' and intends to head South to take up the guise of a preacher or quack healer. But that guise is to go *against the current*. Unwilling to participate in society as it is, Cabot goes underground, to become a secret agent, a subversive Anti-Christ of a world where Bigelow-Martin is polymorphous God, in control of the current.

Eustace Chisholm and the Works draws its material from an earlier phase in the nation's history, the years of the Depression. It is also organised around a writer's attempt to track down the 'real' ingredients of life. The impoverished Eustace spends much of his time writing an epic narrative poem on 'original stock'. He is reduced to using charcoal sticks to emblazon his work across old copies of the Chicago *Tribune*. But the details that lend a historical authenticity simultaneously hint at the novel's concern with the superimposition of universals upon the material world; the narrative of everyday life embodied in the newspapers is overlaid with an old story. The interest in the fate of 'original stock' is the focus of Purdy's work too. The phrase and the act of overlapping one kind of 'language' with another suggest both the subject matter and the formal strategies of his fiction; the lineage of qualities native to America, those rooted in all human history, and the range of art forms that have evolved in relation to both, are all brought to bear on one another. There are many references to 'stock' in *Cabot Wright Begins*, in fact it describes a society which would seem to revolve around the merchandise and imposition of one kind of 'stock' or another. The hero himself gives a comic demonstration of the need for new life to be injected into the national bloodstream, for new strains to be propagated from a depleted species. Even the idea of 'stock figures' takes on a new irony when we consider Purdy's depiction of that world as a giant 'potboiler'. The present novel looks at the era of deprivation which spurred the post-war society to its excesses, its sickening concoction of artificial 'nutrients' and its equation of happiness with consumption.

Just as the previous novel made ironic use of the 'topicality' that was to have been grafted onto the staple fare of the sex novel, so *Eustace Chisholm and the Works* masquerades as a 'period piece'. The naturalistic novel of this epoch with its minute delineation of social conditions purported to mirror 'reality' and collated evidence for its broadly liberal message. But in this case, its characteristics are simulated in order to question its assumptions about human nature and it becomes the vehicle of a very different kind of enquiry. The references to the unemployed, the transients and vagrants that wander the streets, the generalised squalor and the contrasting oases of wealth and privilege, all of which evoke Chicago in the thirties, provide far more than the local colour preliminary to a plea for economic readjustments. Though the author does not exclude the ideological implications of his material, it is viewed through the lens of a much older version of human history. The intersection of different perspectives is mapped out in the opening paragraph:

> Eustace Chisholm's street, with the Home for the Incurables to the south and the streetcar line to the west, extended east up to blue immense choppy Lake Michigan. South of its terminus the great gray museum took up acres and acres with its caryatids, and further south rose the steel mills of Gary and South Chicago with their perpetual vomit of fire. Further down his street in a westerly direction, before Washington Park slipped into the colored ghetto, there was a rose garden in which the German poet, Lessing, sat among the blooms.

The topography suggests Eustace's position at the crossroads of tremendous forces. From the eyrie of his flat he looks out on some vast wheel of fate. The various landmarks are the first in a series of images that are interwoven into the novel's sombre philosophy. The Home for the Incurables introduces a view of life as something akin to a fatal disease; the museum with its acres of caryatids is a reminder of the deadening burden of history; the perpetual vomit of fire from the furnaces anticipates the hellish realm that will be reproduced in the novel's central relationship; lastly, the rose garden, exuding its dream of love and perfection, recalls the idyllic garden of the medieval allegory from which the poet wandered out into the world on his visionary quest.

Eustace's position at the juncture of these forces is dramatised in terms of his involvements with what are almost his 'characters'. His light is left on like some guiding beacon for the chance wanderers of the night. One of his 'disciples', on approaching his building, describes him as God, with his lamp lit, waiting for callers. Indeed, he has acquired a paternal, almost priest-like status in the eyes of the little group that gathers around him. The advice he dispenses might be painful, but there is a grim satisfaction in the truth. He prides himself on being a 'realist' and though the title of the novel's first section, 'The Sun at Noon', derives primarily from the impact of a celestial young man, Amos Ratcliff, it could equally well apply to the discomforting clarity of vision Eustace brings to the fantasies his friends indulge in. But this severity is not just reserved for others. For example, we learn that he is generally known as Ace, and yet, 'The original name, like a scar, he reopened each morning while shaving.'

The various elements in those opening horizons are combined in Eustace's philosophy. He does not see the human wastage and the harshness of his surrounding environment as a temporary economic aberration, indeed, he declares at one point that he has never been interested in anything modern. For him, and for the author one feels, the Depression is simply the current version of history's long mistake. Eustace sees life as something intrinsically flawed in quality, as some flame-like force that works on the combustible material of human dreams. The nation's history would seem to re-capitulate that process. The 'classic American hand', the vessel of 'pure stock' right back to the Indians, that Eustace holds out be-fore his friends, is now trembling like an aspen leaf. It is on the question of love that he differs most strongly from others. His wife, Carla, is typical with her 'American woman's fixed idea that love can cure, love can heal, love can bind a flowing wound'. Yet her voluntary return to the 'penitentiary' where she has to undergo the humiliation of waiting upon Eustace and his new lover, Clay-ton Harms (another child-like wanderer, recalling Bernie Glad-hart), unwittingly endorses her husband's understanding that love and suffering are inextricably entwined. He uses images of drink-ing from a poisoned cup or of having a bacillus in his blood for which science has neither name nor cure to describe his intuition of an ancient and mysterious fatality at the heart of the experi-ence. Thus towards the end of the novel we learn that,

> Carla, *so trained in the rationalism and liberalism of the epoch and partisan to its simple-minded definition of human nature,* finally could only turn away from her husband. She had been able to stand all his other failings, but his having even an unwilling relationship with the 'unknown' began to estrange her at last from him, jeopard-ize her love itself. She thus took refuge in the explanation he was insane. (My italics)

These conflicting views of human nature are dramatised by the novel's narrative movement. It sets up a dialectic between dreams of an ideal, consolatory love and a material world characterised by abortions, disease and squalor. The 'period' background has a similar function to some of the settings in novels by Greene or Conrad. Again, it conjures up the latter's 'destructive element' and continues the feeling of life's promises being soiled and betrayed which runs throughout Purdy's work.

Eustace's philosophy is not as negative as it might seem from such an account, though. He urges his followers to submit themselves to the 'destructive element' and not to hold back from life in the vain hope of preserving their dreams intact. Maureen O'Dell is one of his best 'disciples' in this respect, and it is worth looking at her 'case-history' before examining the novel's major focus on the relationship between his 'main characters', Amos and Daniel. Maureen was 'saved' from her mother and her Christian Science heritage by Eustace's counsels. Her mother and life itself seemed to have conspired to inflict a meaningless suffering upon her. Her 'parent' had abdicated all responsibility; she had feigned ignorance of the meaning of menstrual blood; she gave her daughter no guidance towards the understanding of her sexual identity. Maureen's personal tragedy had been compounded by the twist of fate that had given her the face of a gargoyle on the body of a sylph. Thus her very person is stigmatised with the two colliding forces, beauty and ugliness, that in this novel are a token of life's precarious situation between two extremes. Eustace helps her to give meaning to her suffering by launching her into a 'career' where the two ingredients of joy and pain are intermingled. He insists that if she was ever to find fulfilment as a person and as an artist (her primitive American paintings show an equal interest in 'original stock') then she should give herself unstintingly to the sexual experience, with the intense devotion that had been reserved for her art. The relation between sexual anaesthesia and meretricious literary creation in *Cabot Wright Begins* has its counterpart here. Maureen progresses from being a mere 'coital repeater' (like Carrie) to become a 'partner of love'. Her 'conversion' causes the flowering of a strange attraction that counteracts the disparity of face and body. What is more, her paintings soak up these newly released energies and bring even greater fame and recognition than her vocation as 'serious fucker'!

But Maureen's 'successes' pale before the tragic consequences of the love that would unite Amos and Daniel. It needs to be stressed from the outset, however, that Purdy does not subscribe to those literary stereotypes where 'heterosexual bliss' is pointed up by means of a contrasting 'homosexual agony'. Maureen lives out her own tragedy, she is repeatedly 'skewered and eviscerated, scraped and spooned out, and then not even sewed up but sent home hollow' in the cause of love and is hardly the prototype of the American wife and mother. But neither does the author reverse those literary clichés, for whilst *Cabot Wright Begins* does present a dispassionate and sardonic portrait of heterosexual 'love' in a homophobic society, this next novel can scarcely be construed as a special pleading for the superior pleasures of relationships between members of the same sex. Suffering is seen to be inseparable from all kinds of love. Maureen receives an approbation which has little reference to social structures, she embraces the paradox of love's inevitable agony. Society's codes are just as irrelevant in the severe judgment the novel passes upon Amos and Daniel. They are criticised for failing to be true to their innermost selves; they draw back from life's redeeming experience to bring about a form of destruction which is totally drained of meaning. Though propaganda for minority causes might have been part of the literary model the author resuscitates, the 'case-histories' of the two men become the vehicles of a metaphysical and not a sociological drama. This does not mean that he is not interested in the individual's liberation, but that the obstacles to self-fulfilment are, in his view, more deeply entrenched in human nature.

Daniel Hawes is the landlord of eight shabby rooms at the top of an old building. When he falls in love with Amos Ratcliffe, one of his lodgers, he thinks of it as the last in the long series of disasters that had been his life. It is quickly apparent that Daniel's inability to give expression to that love involves far more than any internalisation of societal prejudices. He is a man who has never wanted to believe in life's possibilities; he has perfected a self that centres uniquely upon the struggle for bodily survival in a harsh environment. Daniel's past is presented as a cameo of the Depression era. Coming from a long line of coal miners, all sense of his individual existence had been subsumed under his family's economic distress and eventual disintegration. He once heard his mother describe him as the kind of boy that nobody ever thought to give a nickname to. His spell in the Army continued to deprive him of this individual 'name'. Subsequently, Chicago swallows him up in its 'industrial whirlwind', leaving him 'free to lie in alleys, sleep on doorsteps or elevated trains, free to panhandle, sink, die, but free'. Yet Daniel survives, thanks to his inbred resilience, his physical strength and perfection, qualities that mark him out as the inheritor of America's 'original stock'. Amos tells him at one point that he likes to look at an American face and Eustace, although it may be wishful thinking on his part, likes to think of Daniel as having some Indian blood in him. But the kind of 'home' he secures for himself has to be propped up by the rigid exclusion of all sentiment, he tries to contain his despair in the only contours he has known:

> The only things which held him to life after his separation from the service had been his Army clothes, his barracks bag, his shoe brush, and his military routine, until Amos. Even now, alone with him in the empty rooms, he felt that they were in the Army together, and that he was Amos's sergeant.

He goes through existence like an automaton, attempting to sever that part of himself that would hope in the face of pain. It is a futile task, however, for although he scrubs his flesh as only a man who hates himself can, as Eustace puts it, nothing can subdue that body's inward aspiration to give and receive love. The absolute divisions he has effected in his psyche are seen in the complete contradictions of his daytime and nighttime behaviour. Although he had scarcely even known the names of his earlier boarders, Daniel sleepwalks into Amos's room at night to bestow blind caresses upon him, acting out the tenderness that is so puritanically denied in his daily routine. Instead of vouching for his 'authenticity', his presentation as the archetypal character of the naturalistic novel becomes an image of his attempt to internalise that genre's disregard for the world of the spirit and for the sense of a mystery in life which transcends the social or economic structures of the moment.

The references to Amos's past scarcely fit in with the 'period' flavour of Daniel's. He seems to be in the 'wrong book', if not the 'wrong world'. Eustace can never get used to the idea that an obscure 'crossroads' should have produced a youth with the celestial imprint of a Greek God, whose dazzling looks have the same effect upon the retinae as 'The Sun at Noon'. There are many hints at his emanation from another realm, at one point he is likened to Pan and indeed he seems like a left-over from some ancient pastoral romance, suddenly thrust into the filth and misery of a depressed urban environment. 'Exile' from the perfect home was repeated in Chicago when Amos's impoverishment resulted in his exclusion from the university. His study of Ancient Greek is in keeping with his origins in antiquity and suggestive of those spiritual dimensions that seek contact with the present world. Whereas Daniel had never known childhood, Amos seemed to have known nothing else, until his rural idyll was brought to an abrupt close by the 'unintentional' sexual relation with Cousin Ida. The incident, precipitated by Amos's rejection by the father who had never deigned to acknowledge his existence with more than idle curiosity, forced the revelation that Ida was his mother. He had been denied the material facts of his identity just as Maureen O'Dell had. Deprived of its connection to the outer world, the perfect love turns back upon itself. Eustace recreates this sense of a dream-like self-containment in his description of this first home:

> . . . camouflaged by hollyhocks, dwarf sunflowers, morning glories, and wild plum trees. Little sea shells bloomed in the garden, frilled snowy curtains hung behind the tiny windows, notes to the milkman stood in bottles on the back steps, clothes lines swayed, birds galore hopped about in the lettuce, mint and sweetpeas, and there that beautiful boy lived, a bastard brought up more lovingly than an heir.

If Daniel had never acquired an individual 'name' due to his circumscription by impersonal structures, Amos is like one of Pirandello's 'characters', an essence, or spirit, in search of the 'author' of its worldly shape. The type of perfection each man embodies is an abstraction from that mutual qualification of 'dream' and 'material reality' that Eustace recommends and the novel as a whole endorses. Neither can survive without entering into relation with the qualities the other possesses; each has been 'schooled' in only one side of life. If Daniel is the descendant of one kind of 'original stock', then Amos is the vehicle of an even older ingredient of history. The latter wanders out into the world like some allegoric figure from the rose garden imaged at the novel's opening. Thus Purdy uses a different type of literary form to depict the 'case-history' of each man, in such a way that their respective situations at the poles of naturalism and allegory carry a metaphysical charge. It suggests that far from yearning for some Platonic realm of pure being, the author sees life to acquire its only meaning from the possible dialectic between these two extremes.

But although the ingredients are brought together, 'nothing' happens. The title of this first section evokes the superstition that at noon, bereft of a shadow, the devil has power over man. Neither Amos nor Daniel have this human 'shadow' and a doom-laden atmosphere builds up around them. We are told that the latter had 'a compact of blood, bone, flesh—that was the target attracting destruction', a notion that is equally applicable to Amos's purity. It is as if fate singles them out with a special fury for holding themselves back from life. Their conversations are fraught with tension and show Purdy's supreme skill in suggesting the terrifying pain of what goes *unsaid*. For example, in the midst of a lecture on Amos's self-neglect, his landlord blurts out, 'Suppose you want to show the world you're tough in spite of your peachbloom face,' and we are told that 'he paused on the word *peachbloom* as if it was this quality he would tear from all creation'. The aura of youthful hope and beauty eats away at the premises he has founded his existence on, the 'scaffolding of his life was falling'. The subsequent course of their love is contained in the image of a promise being torn from all creation. Daniel, with his ingrained bitterness and suspicion, wants to annihilate the deceit he feels the world to be practising upon him. Thus instead of the 'birth' of new life, we have prophetic anticipations of the 'death' that is to fall prematurely upon the two men. Premonitions of their doom are filtered obliquely through their relationships with Eustace and Maureen O'Dell.

Eustace, like some master of ceremonies, urges them both to the brink of confession, insisting that they give themselves up to the present moment and accept life's gift of love since time will inevitably bring about its destruction. He is like the ghost of Andrew Marvell inciting his coy lovers to make haste! But neither of them has the courage to speak his feeling in the 'daylight' world and so the 'abortion' of that love comes to have its grotesque image in Maureen's 'payday'. The unwanted offspring of one of Daniel's routine soldierly fornications is symbolically linked to Amos himself. The reverberations of the title, 'The Sun at Noon', are concentrated in the fatality of this scene. It is presided over by a macabre doctor, 'black as the ace of spades and twice as baleful', and scrutinised with a merciless clarity of vision. It is a savage mockery of 'creation', a horrifying close-up on a sacrifice without meaning. As the battered and decapitated foetus is being withdrawn, Amos falls and cuts his head open:

> Whether it was the sight of so much blood flowing as far as his shoes, or the strange insane shock that the amniotic sac had to do with Greek for little lamb, the room shot up before him, and then swam in sickening blackness as he fell heavily to the floor.

'I saw baby's broken head,' his 'mother' declares when it is all over, referring not to the material shape of Daniel's 'manhood' but to Amos himself. The whole scene foreshadows the concluding images of the novel where, true to Maureen's prophecy, Daniel is put on the cross, to be 'skewered and drawn and quartered'. There are many instances of love's betrayal being projected in terms of an evasion of parenthood. Amos is finally driven out of his preferred home by his landlord's failure to intercede in the outright 'purchase' of his celestial visitor by another man, Reuben Masterson. Daniel enters the vacated room with the trepidation of a parent straying into the abode of a dead child; he puts a soiled shirt to his lips. The bundle of letters from Cousin Ida that he discovers form an ironic commentary upon his own abdication. His tardiness is framed by Ida's pleas for Amos to come home; she says the years are running out. Dwelling on the past, she laments, 'if only he had looked after you as a real father should . . .'.

From this point Amos and Daniel move further and further into their separate realms. The narrative movement describes the opening of a tremendous fissure that folds them both back into the timeless flow of non-being. The love that promised to bind them together is torn asunder as each enters into a perverse form of 'marriage'. Amos ascends to a 'heavenly' zone, presided over by the God-like Reuben Masterson; Daniel, meanwhile, descends to a hellish domain to embrace what Eustace describes as his 'dark bridegroom', the Army. Amos's comic progress towards the city's underworld is sombrely counterpointed by Daniel's imprisonment and torture 'Under Earth's Deepest Stream', as the last section is entitled. But though they appear to move in contrary directions, both are engulfed by essentially the same sea of dissolution. As with *Cabot Wright Begins*, rigid structures come to be interchangeable with the shapelessness of the ocean stream. Thus, when Daniel has the idea of returning to the womb of the Army, 'the word "re-enlistment" came over him like a wave of sea water' and he is excited to the point of having an erection. Amos, likewise, is 'adrift in a sea' and his Cousin Ida's fears and premonitions with regard to his being a poor swimmer and drowning are borne out by the course of events. Their hallucinatory journeys are drawn together by hints and parallels to the Ancient Mariner's betrayal of God's sign, though in this case there is no ultimate redemption. Their breach of faith similarly brings down some dreadful curse upon their heads, as they act out the larger failings of the encompassing society. The matriarch of that world, old Mrs Masterson, decides, somewhat confusedly, that Amos is her 'albatross'! Each has a foreboding of some 'nameless' terror bearing down upon him, and each finds a momentary respite before the final act. Amos is temporarily solaced in the arms of the old lady's gardener, whilst Daniel rejoices to see a living creature stray across the path that leads to his torture.

When Reuben Masterson offers himself as guardian to the fragile spirit of love we see another strand in the pattern of national failure. He bears the imprint of the native tradition whereby a few families accumulate vast wealth at everybody else's expense. He is the scion of one of the great 'front' families, an apt denomination for the splendiferous façade that conceals vacuity. 'Mucilaged' together by money, he is another of those characters whose whole existence is subsumed under a 'name'. He merely pays lip-service to the ideal of love, as is evident when Amos is dressed in princely garments and endlessly apostrophised, before being deposited in the family 'vaults' (otherwise known as old Mrs Masterson) whilst Reuben goes off to worship 'Bacchus' in the great city, The effect Amos produces upon the era's *grande dame* is revealing; when she first sets eyes on him, we are told that 'She felt an irresistible wish to touch even to pet the young man, and at the same time an overmastering urge to order him from the house.' Furthermore, in the confusion of the moment, she almost decides to make him her heir. Amos is like the memory of the life she has exiled herself from, the spectre of the outside world she has kept at bay. Yet at the same time, she dimly recognises that the empire she has carefully garnered would be dissipated if she opened the door to those hungry phantoms. Though she yearns for the perpetuation of the family name, Mrs Masterson's single-minded devotion to material goals has deprived her grandson of the ability to form loving relationships with members of either sex. There are many ironies as Amos and his patrons bring about their mutual destruction. Whilst the youth loses all sense of his ever precarious identity, various documents connected with his past bring the old matriarch into contact with the different faces of the love she has outlawed. Having procured herself a copy of Xenophon's *Banquet*, a book Amos has been rather pointedly buried in, she then comes across Cousin Ida's letters and a memoir entitled 'Visits from a Sleepwalker'. The dizzying impact of these revelations comes to a climax when the door of her gardener's cottage is flung open upon a Bacchanalian scene that causes her heart to fail. After his expulsion from the household, Amos declines rapidly. Dressed like a character out of the Arabian Nights, he disappears into the city's netherworld, surrendering his body to its loveless denizens. He dies absurdly, shot as a burglar, as he is coming out of the house of the clairvoyant whose 'mantle' had fallen like a curse upon Eustace. The latter had charged him to procure enough money to exorcise this unwanted gift, but it is Amos himself who is exorcised in a final case of *mistaken identity*.

There is a perfect symmetry in the shape given to Amos's and Daniel's fate: whilst the former is clothed only in the outward guises of love, the latter undergoes a bodily disintegration that travesties the sexual union of two men. The dream world is thus interwoven with messages from a realm that is as nightmarish as something out of Edgar Allan Poe. Daniel meets his fate through the 'offices' of Captain Stadger, the demonic counterpart of Reuben Masterson. Amos provides the key to this final section when he remarks bitterly that his landlord returned to the Army to save himself the trouble of committing suicide. On the very night of his arrival at the camp, Daniel sleepwalks into the officer's tent. Afterwards, when he hears the name 'Stadger', he utters a low cry as if 'his body knew something which he could not define, and it had cried out just now with his voice'. It is made abundantly clear that Captain Stadger is not a personification of the meaningless suffering the world inflicts upon its helpless victims, but the shape Daniel has *chosen* to give life. His body's subconscious knowledge finds its definition in their relationship. The course of events recapitulates Daniel's situation of his being at one extreme of life; his inability to believe in anything but a meaningless pain is imaged by the way he seeks out the 'army' within the Army. His presentation of his body for 'duty' in the officer's tent denotes his submission to that force that he feels has dogged him throughout life, and anticipates the final stage where he hunts down his persecutor.

Gradually Daniel is relieved of all routine duties to become the single conscript in Stadger's private army. In ghostly settings, alive with memories of Indians, childhood picnics and other tokens of a collective past that promised a less harrowing future, the two men perform a macabre version of those ceremonies announced in the newspaper clipping that brought Daniel face to face with the death of his love. Its headline read: 'Funeral Rites For Slain Youth.'

Stadger is like Daniel's double, his secret self. It is as if each had conjured the other out of the depths of his being as the final exorcist of that body's tormenting aspirations. Each provides the perfect instrument for the other to express his ingrained despair. The sleepwalking soldier inspires his officer with a vision of 'fulfilled hope', the answer to all his dreams. Similarly, 'the most exquisite torment he could have ever imagined his body capable of in his wildest imaginings' is procured in Daniel when the 'nameless' instruments of torture are thrust into him. He takes a grim satisfaction on being 'so hideously injured by Stadger for no purpose or meaning. It confirmed somehow everything he felt about man and life.' Thus pain is taken to such an extreme that it offers a blissful release from the struggle to understand the suffering that is part of life. We are told that tears were not Daniel's forte and he was grateful he could bleed. Stadger is clung to as his 'anaesthetician' and the 'hook' that engendered a release from the difficulties of selfhood in *Cabot Wright Begins*, has its grotesque equivalent.

The horror and lingering impact of these events stems not so much from the details of physical suffering, but from the terrible ironies attached to the fact that they testify simultaneously to the force of the love that is intended to be annihilated as a possibility. Both men have a physical beauty that contradicts their version of life. Furthermore, though on one level Daniel's sleepwalking into his officer's tent denotes the seeking out of his executioner, on another level his rebellious body is making the same plea for love that Amos was confronted with. Stadger not only resembles Amos at times but he contains the same fierce longing to give himself to the soldier. Neither man can eradicate these aspirations, they can only become partners in suicide. Even though Daniel is brought to relive the underground hell of his coal mining days, the belief in love clings on despite his refusal to act upon it. This is deftly imaged when Stadger, who at heart wants to be preferred to Amos, elicits a testimonial to love from his 'secret-sharer' that comes in a voice 'as deep as if it had risen from the bottom of a shaft'. The tremendous tensions that build up between them are not simply engendered by the despair of the proceedings but by the possibility that at any moment they will give way to the attraction it feeds on. There are moments when they lie together amongst flowers, like two exhausted lovers. More significantly, their self-destructive impulses are channelled through some of the very acts that denote love and dedication between two men. The merging of souls symbolised in the blood-letting ceremony of *blutbruderschaft* takes on a horrific literality as their chests are slashed in a frenzied compact of self-annihilation, just as the final act of penetration and disembowelment is a cruel mockery of the sexual union.* With such scenes of bloody carnage the wheel comes full circle and the 'abortion' of love is complete.

* There is an interesting essay by Roger Austen that compares the degree of stereotyping and implicit judgments of homosexuality in works by Melville, Lawrence, Carson McCullers, Dennis Murphy and Purdy. He argues persuasively that only Carson McCullers and Purdy allow their compassion for all types of love to be expressed openly: 'But for fate and ban: Homosexual Villains and Victims in the Military', Special Issue of *College English*, *The Homosexual Imagination*, Vol. 36, No. 3 (November 1974).

The wider significance of this failure is expressed in the changes that take place in Eustace. His literary enterprise thrives, to begin with, as he pours all communications from or about the ill-starred lovers into the Works. Having always been 'queer' for paper, the discovery of 'real' letters that spoke with the 'authentic, naked, unconcealed voice of love' inspired in him an enthusiasm usually reserved for 'blood'. Thus the correspondence of Daniel Hawes and Cousin Ida is greeted as an unexpected stroke of luck. But as he drinks in the full bodied 'stock' of life and literature, Eustace comes to think of himself, rather ominously, as being 'hooked' only on Daniel's story. The precedence the one correspondent takes over the other suggests a fracturing in the dialectic of hope and despair that had at least been promised life in his art. Cousin Ida stirs hopeful memories in many of the characters at some point or another and she is almost alone in her ability to speak of the suffering involved in love without a loss of belief. Yet the two subjects, Amos and Daniel, that Eustace had thought of as 'one' are now deprived of the axis of faith. He quickly loses interest in his narrative poem as the artist's vision becomes a 'curse' that he longs to be cured of. The whole USA is 'nothing but Daniels and Amoses whispering and muttering to him in the falling darkness'. Having achieved his popularity as someone who was always willing to listen, Eustace now wants to shut his ears, like that friend of Cousin Ida for whom there were some things that were too terrible to be spoken aloud. He wants to get off the 'hook' of being human, but, as we see when Amos is shot in the attempt to free him of the 'mantle' passed on by the negro psychic, he can do so only at the expense of one of his main characters.

Whereas Eustace gives in to despair, Purdy with his masterful dialogue between comic and tragic elements reconciles those extremes. As with Zoe Bickle, Eustace's failure as a writer is an extension of his failure as an individual. Once a 'figure' that stood out against the historical background, he shies away from the pain of telling the 'real' story, abdicates as guardian of 'original stock', shrinks in stature and fades away into his surroundings. His narrative poem goes up in flames to coincide with the conflagration of human hopes in society's larger 'economic burnout'. In a novel that seeks its own definitions of manhood, Eustace's final turning to his long-suffering wife does not necessarily imply that he has seen some heterosexual 'light'. On the contrary, it seems more like the action of a child seeking comfort in his mother. Purdy insists to the last that there is no escape; the subject Eustace flees is part of him, for what he offers Carla is still 'a kind of *ravening* love'.

4

The House of the Solitary Maggot and Jeremy's Version

Sleepers in Moon-Crowned Valleys reveals the author's increasing absorption in the workings of memory and the process of age. It also continues his own history of the American soul by examining the impingement of a more distant past upon the present. Whereas the two novels dealt with in the previous chapter form a commentary upon recent phases in national history and define themselves in ironic relation to a genre of literature associated with each, this novel sequence evokes an earlier era and its chronicles of successive generations enter into a dialogue with the art forms of nostalgia.

Jeremy's Version (1970) and *The House of the Solitary Maggot* (1974) are described as a 'continuous novel', though their relation is contrapuntal rather than sequential. Each develops a variant upon that phenomenon imaged in the overall title whereby the American psyche would seem destined to sleep on forever, in truly lunar madness, substituting dreams for reality. Both novels encapsulate story within story as successions of narrators feed parasitically upon the body of the past. 'Only the foetus lives in the present' is how one of the characters in *Jeremy's Version* puts it. There are differences too, the most noticeable being that *The House of the Solitary Maggot* presents a starker, more intense version of its predecessor. The perspective lent by the psychological landscape of the small town gives way to a remoter locality where primal energies erupt in a world more dream-like and more acutely enclosed upon itself.

Both novels are initially framed by a description of how the

overall narrator is captured and taken over by the enchantment of
a past where giant-like personages are caused to re-enact their
parts in a lost world. Both figures are so absorbed by this reconstruction that their 'terrestial' links are severed. Admittedly, as far
as Jeremy was concerned, there were few roots to secure him in
present-day Boutflour. At the threshold of the adult world, his
cross-tempered half-sister, Della Gassman, is his only guide. Her
crabby lectures on bad company can do nothing to prevent his
falling prey to a local eccentric, Matt Lacey, whose skill in evok-
ing the tempestuous saga of the Ferguses casts a spell over him.
The House of the Solitary Maggot advertises its self-containment
in an even more emphatic fashion. The plaque above Eneas Har-
mond's doorway bears the legend 'DO NOT DISTURB'—the novel's
opening words. Just as Matt Lacey (the town's leading ghost,
according to Jeremy) shuts himself off from modern Boutflour
within his crumbling mansion, so the characters in this subsequent
narrative close the door upon the contemporary world. Eneas had
renounced everything to take up residence in Nora Bythewaite's
fortress of memories, a stronghold which is penetrated only
occasionally by the sharper of the local rumours. He declares that
some dreadful inadequacy in the present epoch has riven them
backwards into the past.

The opening to each novel, then, is like a ceremony during
which the insubstantial identities on offer in the present society
are cast off before a defiant retreat into the domain of memory.
The chorus of vituperation directed at the modern age would seem
designed to enhance and set off the recollections of a more colourful way of life, one that has been bulldozed away in the cause of
a specious progress. Roots and traditions have been swept into
oblivion before the great deity of commerce. Matt claims, for instance, that 'the only talented and original people the town ever
had were driven out, ridden on a rail, tarred and feathered', whilst
Eneas laments that the small community of Prince's Crossing 'no
longer exists, expunged by a merciless state, county and township
authority'. The 'great-nephew' who shares Eneas's preferences has
even taken on a vow of silence in view of what he regards to be the
nation's crimes at home and abroad. Such wholesale flight before
the voracious materialism that converts everything in its path into
a drab uniformity might seem a healthy reaction, setting the scene

for the novel of romantic escapism, the 'family saga in the classic fireside tradition', as one of the cover writers for *Jeremy's Version* would have us believe.

But these first impressions prove deceptive; the clear cut boundaries between past and present soon begin to dissolve. At times the narrators would appear to have been created by the very spirits offered as compensation for their rootlessness. For example, Matt feels there is nothing fortuitous about his meeting with Jeremy. He quickly divines the newspaper boy's predilection for 'out-of-fashion fiction' and conveys the invitation to become 'one of us' with a weary satisfaction at his 'improbable' visitor. Jeremy's appointment as 'ammanuensis' suggests his transformation to the appendage of some more dominant entity, especially when we find he resembles Jethro, one of the principal characters in the Fergus saga, and comes to utter streams of words from some inner world beyond his comprehension. He is even stabbed 'inadvertently' over the heart with a paper knife before being promoted to the office of 'secretary to the dead'! The opening pages of *The House of the Solitary Maggot* disclose similar ambivalences. Eneas muses over the mysterious arrival of the 'great-nephew' and suspects that avowed relationship to have been 'invented'. When he tries to elicit his name, Nora only bursts out laughing and declares, 'He is entirely impossible, Eneas, but I am not in need of a *possible* young man.' It transpires that some of the stranger's distinguishing traits have been inherited from two of her 'sons', Owen and Aiken. The allusions to his 'great luminous, if going blind, eyes' and to his unwashed condition, 'like a horse', point to an amalgamation of their characteristics. Even our sense of Eneas as a 'real' person is gradually disturbed. The 'great-nephew', breaking his vow of silence, assails him ghoulishly with the question 'If I could have some of the marrow like from your bones, do you think I could get through the rest of it . . . my life?' When Eneas lets slips references to his own hereditary weakness of the eyes, we are able to associate this with his legendary strength, his war wound, and Nora's propensity for losing 'sons', to see that his autonomy is caught up within some weird pattern of fate.

Thus the frame that seemed calculated to throw a favourable light upon the reconstruction of a Golden Age has something curious, even sinister, about its shut-in quality. It causes a warning shadow to fall across the persons of Jeremy and Eneas. Their solidity, their youth and homely warmth have been slowly sapped, as if they had come into the presence of death. In fact, Matt speaks of his 'subject' as 'the only thing that kept him from the cold clay of the grave', whilst Nora jubilantly exclaims of her 'great-nephew' that 'instead of death, he came'. The 'subject' that procures the sensation of outwitting time can be taken to refer both to the corpus of memories that keeps them alive and to those human bodies whose ensnarement seems necessary for the past to re-assert itself. As sole survivors of the sagas they were part of, Matt and Nora delight in exercising a retrospective omniscience over their stories. But as is frequently the case in Purdy's work, the act of narration (the one-way 'message') is seen to have become the substitute for loving relationships and respect for individual identities. In this way we are given the first intimations that 'life' transmits itself along channels that have by-passed such positive qualities. The 'family resemblances' acquired by the various young men spring from some kind of 'artificial insemination'.

The encroachment of one narrative layer upon another, or of the past upon the present, simulates a fictitious world preying on a 'real' one. The sense of a diminishing reality that disturbs our impressions of the overall narrators accelerates when the substance of those memories is reproduced in detail. The refusal to participate in the present world that circumscribes the proliferating inner stories turns out to be their only content. We come to see that nowhere in the past did Matt or Nora really come to terms with life. Their present artistry mirrors the way their whole lives were dreamed away in attempts to impose 'versions' upon a recalcitrant reality. Memory in these two novels is not so much the repository of genuine feelings but the means of manufacturing dreams in reverse.

But despite the doubts that accrue around the overall narrators' reliability, their homely and idiomatic speech patterns act as filters and perform an unwitting commentary upon the fantastic happenings imparted to them. Furthermore, the narrative outpourings of the various characters are refracted through Purdy's own complex ironies and image systems. We are led to suspect the value attached to this lost world as each attempt to 'fix' it causes its magic to recede even further into the past. We encounter fiction within fiction until 'reality' disappears in a sort of infinite regression, or so it seems at first.

One of the more obvious ways in which the author suggests this endemic escapism is to conjure up his own spirits from the past. In particular, there are many allusions to that first American dreamer—Rip Van Winkle. Leslie Fiedler's account of this archetypal figure and its spectral hold upon the literary imagination is well known.* But Purdy's references to the giant of native mythology are not contrived in any way when one considers his cumulative endeavour to chart the ancestry of the national psyche. The patriarchal skeleton in the family cupboard is a natural, if ironic, metaphor since so much of his work treats disturbances within family relationships, on one level at least, as miniatures of national phenomena.

The 'husband' in each of the two families portrayed reincarnates Rip's familiar aversion to domesticity and responsibility. In *Jeremy's Version* Matt tells how Wilders Fergus, having married Elvira and lost their combined fortunes, was forever absenting himself from home. On the rare occasions when he did return, he managed unfailingly to father a son upon his wife. He became a dream-sick pioneer on the frontier of speculative finance, fleeing from the disappointments time had unfolded and closing his eyes to a world which contradicted his youthful vision of life's promise. One of his sons, Jethro, thinks of him with unconscious irony as someone he had read of in a child's story book. Wilders himself reflects that 'he had been gone it would seem longer than Rip Van Winkle and he found the world more changed than that old failure had'. But whereas his legendary counterpart profited from his absence, Wilders is doomed to remain a wanderer, like a bewildered left-over (echoing his name) from one of the Fenimore Cooper novels which constituted his preferred reading. Time has stopped for him in the sense that all development as a person has been arrested; he has exiled himself from life's possibilities by refusing to acknowledge any power greater than his own ego and by subordinating all human relationships to the pursuit of the 'Gilded

* Leslie Fiedler, *The Return of the Vanishing American* (Cape, 1969).

Age's Gods'—those glories of wealth and position he had once glimpsed.

The legacy of his fall from grace and his flight from responsibility is imaged somewhat grotesquely when Jethro slips from an orchard tree to be impaled on the iron spikes of the railings. Like Irving's Rip, whose fences were always falling to pieces, Wilder's vague resolution to go home to 'mend fences' was somewhat belated. Jethro's 'accident' depicts the inability of both parents to face up to suffering, for whilst Elvira weeps perfunctorily, Wilders confines himself to mumbling phrases heard long ago. Only on one occasion does he reassert himself as a man and father, when Jethro witnesses his fight with someone his financial schemes had ruined. For once, the elegant, though old-fashioned, nonentity, whose very perspiration seemed odourless, opts to confront an adversary. After a ferocious battle, during which the outer tokens of identity are ripped to shreds, Jethro has the sensation of 'walking with a man he had never before known and someone who was clothed it seemed only in blood and stains from vegetation and earth'. But the man of flesh and blood soon creeps back into his shell. He recoils in particular from the aggression of his womenfolk, or as Jethro puts it: 'Between the two of them, Mama and Aunt Winifred, they've done a clean good thorough job of snipping off Wilders' balls.'

The 'father' in *The House of the Solitary Maggot* is more distant than Wilders even. At least there was no doubt about the latter's fatherhood in a biological sense, whereas Mr Skegg only selectively acknowledges his blood relationship to Nora Bythewaite's children. Like Wilders, he had known great financial success for a brief while, but after the Wall Street Crash he wastes his life trying to regain his former eminence. If he cannot reassert himself as a national figure, then he is determined to exercise his power over Nora, at least. Despite his piercing eyesight, he is quite 'asleep' in his own way. He nurtures miserly dreams of controlling the destinies of those around him, yet he is quite blind to the need his sons might have of him. The ferocity of his will is neatly imaged in the dual connotations of the word; he constantly rewrites that document as if he aimed to prescribe the future as well. The estrangement of both fathers from their sons and from life itself is summed up by the image of Jethro at the end of *Jeremy's Version*. He lies in a flower bed at the Fergus home, like a sacrificial object, hoping for death. We are told that 'He heard his father's voice from as great a distance as the eclipsed moon itself.'

The bellicose spirit of Dame Van Winkle lives on in the three principal female characters—Elvira Summerlad and Winifred Fergus in *Jeremy's Version* and Nora Bythewaite in *The House of the Solitary Maggot*. All three seem to aspire towards a degree of self-sufficiency that would relegate the male to the status of eternal son, brother, or temporary sexual companion. None can contemplate the evolution of mature unions between equals. They seem to belong in spirit to the system of pre-hellenic Greece where woman was worshipped as the Great Goddess, the immortal changeless and omnipotent being, who took lovers for pleasure and not to provide any children that might result with a father. Indeed, the concept of fatherhood is supposed to have been initially absent from their religious thought.

It is not long before Elvira discovers great advantages in her husband's protracted absences. One of her closest friends ruminates secretly that 'she had never wanted Wilders to be a father to her boys and that she had her own jealous passion of possessiveness for them which must have resisted from the beginning any encroachment by anybody on her unique role and position of importance in her son's lives.' Though there is no denying the ferocity of her love, Elvira's sons seem primarily important as guarantors of her own youth and beauty. They provide the raw materials from which she constructs an image of an ideal self. She lives like a queen bee at the centre of her male-populated territory, hoping to secure herself a constant flow of adulation. Any movement towards maturity on the part of her sons is resisted as a token of the ageing process which involves her too. As Jethro, who literally bears the scars of the family breakdown, gets belligerent and Rick becomes restive ('. . . must I stay tied to your apron strings forever in this cabbage patch on the river?' is his constant refrain) and Wilders threatens to return, Elvira's 'version' becomes subject to attacks from every quarter. The extent of her egoism is most apparent in the self-pitying reaction to Jethro's 'accident'. It is seen only as a disruption of her golden vistas and we are told that 'the disappointment of life bore down on her as if she too had fallen from a height onto spines.'

Winifred Fergus battles with equal ferocity to control the lives of all the menfolk in her family and has even decided to wrest her three nephews from Elvira's custody. Her blistering tongue is frequently in service—faced with her brother's misdemeanours: 'Winifred was judge, jury, supreme court, she lectured, accused, gave what paltry defense could be picked out of such irresponsibility and monumental wickedness and then in a ringing cry that seemed to come from some bird of prey in the skies, found him guilty on all counts.' But as with Elvira, the granite-like exterior is vulnerable to attack from 'within'. Her spurious morality crumbles under the impact of Jethro's journal. At the moment of what ought to have been one of her greatest triumphs, she is given a horrifying glimpse of the real self she had buried. Beneath the shrewish mask, she is ablaze with envy. Elvira has achieved the self-sufficiency she aspires to; her various needs would appear to be gratified without any sacrifice of her autonomy; having dispensed with the trouble of a husband, her sons supply her with love and her entourage of lodgers with sexual pleasure. Before she can *recompose* herself, Winifred is assailed by a vision of the household where 'unfettered love and ecstasy and every unrestraint had gone on so without a husband and father to hold back the tide of it all'.

Nora Bythewaite in *The House of the Solitary Maggot* is cast in the same mould. She fights endlessly to safeguard her own independence whilst combatting the bids for freedom in others. In her 'dream of life' she had refused to believe that her sons would ever leave home or that she would grow old. Scornful of the destinies of common women, she had felt able to rearrange the 'ancient pattern' in accordance with her own desires. Her resistance to the flow of time is seen, for example, when the incident of Aiken giving Owen his first shave is transformed in her mind to a ceremony where they both frolicked around her open casket. It seems apt that the cyclone that devastates the neighbourhood should have been dubbed locally as 'Lady Bythewaite'. The whole countryside bears the marks for many years afterwards, 'there are whole forests there which lie pigmy stunted and dead from the maniacal hands of the whirling winds'. The psychological landscape around Nora is equally scarred.

Rip Van Winkle is not the only spirit the author conjures up from the past to insinuate the pernicious effects of these attempts to arrest the flow of time and to regain some lost world. The myth-making capacities of his characters are subverted by allusions to other patterns of fate they unwittingly repeat. Not only do many of them belong in spirit to the feudal company of the Greek Gods, but they also rehearse one of antiquity's best remembered legends, that of Oedipus. Both parts of the 'continuous novel' are pervaded with evidence of blindness. For example, Nora and her sons actually carry the stigma of this mythic ancestor in their common defects of eyesight. Little wonder she is thought of as a 'legend' in the neighbourhood, for her tendency to 'lose' or 'overlook' sons is quite extraordinary. Whilst she is busily congratulating herself on having 'invented' Owen's name and indeed his life, just as Mr Skegg ungraciously suggests she has her own, Nora is reduced to the status of a character in somebody else's book when 'fate' springs an attack from an unexpected quarter. Aiken, whose name suggests his craving for love, is 'fate's child', the nemesis upon which his mother is 'impaled', the contradiction of those assumptions that she could immunise herself from life's tragedies, a sharp reminder that she had 'forgotten' herself. When Nora finally allows herself to recognise the son who has re-enacted the role of Oedipus, she also comes ironically close to identifying the author who opposes her reduction of life to a fiction. She muses that 'perhaps Aiken had come straight from God, that he had no mortal father after all, but that she had become pregnant with him by some unknown whirling force and he was her punishment and judgment'.

The incorporation of these myths suggests the endless circularity of experience. They are also part of a more extensive network of imagery, revolving around dualities such as 'blindness' and 'vision', 'sleep' and 'reality', that gives both narratives their strange, dream-like texture. The underlying symbolic patterns are drawn together by specific references to the various media of illusion—the theatre, the cinema, the novel, in fact to any of the 'languages' that give shape to the imagination.

This is seen in *Jeremy's Version* when Rick rejects the identity circumstances thrust upon him to seek out a more glamorous role. He tries to extract himself from the depressing shabbiness of the boarding house, the 'mud-puddle' that masquerades as a town and his family. He refashions his living quarters with every luxury and divests himself of all provincial mannerisms with the help of

117

drama lessons. He soon becomes the protégé of a little clique of older people who once tasted a more colourful life than Boutflour could offer and who hope to renew their assault upon the portals of fame through Rick. For them, the stage represents the solipsist's paradise, the arena in which identities can be fabricated, the constrictions of selfhood evaded and the encroachment of time postponed. It is reduced to its vulgarest form as a place where the societal ideals of youth and beauty can be deified and worshipped by the 'dream-sick' populace. But although Rick makes sharp divisions between his actual circumstances and the glamour he aspires to, the novel as a whole insists that the stage is, in fact, a microcosm of everyday relationships. The ritual of Elvira's inner table is typical; it provides the stage and audience essential to her reshaping and retelling of past events and the base from which to prescribe and rehearse future developments. It is a carefully constructed sanctuary, set apart from the sparser eating place of the boarders. Furthermore, when her territory is subject to attack from outsiders, Elvida is capable of 'performances' that would make the local Thespians pale into insignificance. For example, when her arch-enemy Winifred bears down upon the household, the two of them enter into a championship match where they are literally fighting to possess their audience. Elvira launches into battle with a salvo resembling 'some great public bulletin coming over the radio to an assembled nation'. When the intruder is finally driven out, Elvira is able to give credit to her fellow actress for the aplomb with which she marches off to demand assistance from the local filling station in regal disregard of her shredded costume and exposed bosoms. Ironically, though, from Rick's point of view, the scene bears no relation whatsoever to his expectations of the 'glitter' required of the theatre. He despairingly identifies 'a gloomy even grimy realism that was defeating to the purposes of real drama' and sighs over the fact that 'one could not make a play or a movie out of what was happening here, it was too small town and shabby'.

Individual performances collide as each struggles to be the sole arbiter of his or her image. In *The House of the Solitary Maggot* the attempts to wrest control of the 'script' are on an even grander scale. The rivalry of the two actresses has its counterpart in the feudal squabbles of the competing 'narrators': Nora Bythewaite and Mr Skegg. From the seclusion of their separate mansions, they try to assert themselves over the surrounding countryside. Territorial claims are similarly advanced and repulsed in the psychological no-man's land which has been created in the lives of their 'sons'. They operate like two lunatic writers, each striving to encapsulate the other's materials or jubilantly recounting an installment the other is ignorant of. For example, when Skegg falls ill due to his frustrated attempts to capture the elusive *word* Nora is reported to have uttered during her 'seizure', not content with pulverising him verbally, she extracts one of his aching teeth in punitive fashion and exultantly probes the underlying abscess to unleash 'a swelling rivulet of pus and foul smelling gouts of blood'. She not only 'maims' him like a 'savage chief', just as she 'scalped' Aiken and 'unmanned' Clarence, but confirms his defeat by cunningly purchasing two of his finest farms during his indisposition.

The blood that flows ritualistically on so many occasions complements the imagery connected with maggots to suggest a tapping of the life-flow itself. Thus when Aiken arrives at Skegg's house, oozing blood, the old maggot is transformed by the unexpected gift of materials from which he can document the weaknesses of others. His leech-like appetite is temporarily satiated, his often irregular heart pumps steadily as he savours the transference of power. He is, of course, serenely oblivious to the real import of the liquid that flows so amply over the pristine paternal floor. The locality's corruption of the word 'magnate' to 'maggot' is an apt designation of his cannibalistic greed. The propensities echoed in Nora's name and the many allusions to Skegg's uncommonly white teeth and piercing eyesight suggest that both aspire to the status of 'the solitary maggot'. This central image recalls William Golding's *Pincher Martin* where the protagonist's philosophy in life might be summed up in the notion 'eat or be eaten'. Great emphasis is placed upon another character's account of a Chinese practice whereby a box containing a fish would be buried until the occupant's flesh had been devoured by maggots and they had reduced themselves to a solitary, bloated specimen which would then be disinterred to become the prey of an even larger appetite. The form of Purdy's novel is like that of Golding's in so far as the 'patterns' their central characters would impose on the world are caught up and eventually demolished by the workings of more inclusive 'patterns'. In Purdy's case, the strange surface texture of his novel is produced by the continual reverberations of such colliding images and versions.

At first it might seem that endless collisions would result only in a total erasure of meaning, taking us back to that ubiquitous 'wall'. Each character would seem to have been negated by Rip's inherited estrangement. They all take up some position on the periphery of life whilst being tormented by the idea that 'reality' awaits them elsewhere. The compulsion to escape the difficulties of selfhood in the present takes the form of projecting an ideal or dream of fulfilment onto some other time, place or relationship. For example, Matt Lacey worships Elvira from afar, but even though he is telegrammed imperiously to come 'home' he can only take up the role of honorary 'son' and must continue to pay homage to that projection of his own imagined needs. Whilst he yearns to be completely on the 'inside' of the family circle, Rick, the eldest son, longs to be on the 'outside', to take up the very career Matt has renounced. Similarly, in *The House of the Solitary Maggot* we encounter a variety of characters who aspire to be part of the very relationships that others find intolerable. Nora's 'great-nephew' is reputed to have scoured the land for a relative with such parasitic fervour that it is rather apt for Eneas to mistake the word 'tape-recorder' for 'tapeworm'. When Aiken is trying to escape Nora's household, he is advised by the lonely young cinema manager, Stephen Bottrell, who is as hypnotised by The Family as Matt, to stay where he 'belongs' unless he wants to find himself in the 'real canyons for the buried alive'. There would appear to be an infinite number of versions, as if 'real' life disappeared in a sequence of mirrors, of proscenium frames or of chinese boxes. Thus we find that even when Matt Lacey would appear to have added the final layers of drama to the saga of Elvira's family, drawing upon his talents as actor and ventriloquist, there is still Jeremy to be reckoned with, not to mention the insertions and corrections his half-sister is determined on. Still further, there are rumours that the last 'stage' may not be here even; Matt seems to have set his heart on some kind of revival at the former 'Grand Opera House'!

We do not altogether suffocate in a welter of 'fictions'. Purdy retaliates with his own 'counter-performances' so that we are tuned into a duet rather than a monotonous rumbling of collapsing structures. There are certain characters who provide glimpses of the 'real' world that has been glossed over. Jethro in *Jeremy's Version* and Owen and Aiken in *The House of the Solitary Maggot* bring us directly into contact with the 'inside story' of suffering and love.

At first Jethro tries to reconcile himself to neglect by constructing compensatory stories. Never having experienced the life in Hittisleigh that his mother retrospectively endows with all the charms of Eden and holds to be the very antithesis of present-day Boutflour, he tells himself that 'Rick and Elvira were angels of the damned legion who were assigned to torture him while above, on earth, in Hittisleigh, lived the true Elvira and Wilders who mourned their lost son.' But the extremity of his pain causes even these desperate fantasies to crumble. He is the only one to face up to the horrifying vacuum and absence of love at the centre of the family. Indeed, he is the very personification and product of that 'absence'. Jethro documents his mother's whoring and his brother's narcissistic prostitution of himself with an agonized frankness. His journal seems to wield the 'scalpel of the doctor of autopsy stripping each piece of skin from those who had so much as stepped in front of his gaze.' In fact, like Warburton's Sermons in *Cabot Wright Begins*, this is also the effect it has upon those encapsulating narrative layers. Though the journal is still a 'version', it is one which exposes rather than one which obscures and its explosive impact upon other characters is enough to endorse the notion that a 'reality' has been transcribed. Though Wilders tries to persuade himself that it is an image of Jethro's accident or his current depravity, his view of the likely effect upon his sister only vouches for its authenticity.

> Winifred hated, he was aware, 'nature', sweat, pain, sickness, madness, heavy breathing and tears, sorrow and death—all the things that had to do with blood, and the journals of Jethro, though weird and exaggerated at times, underlined everybody's relationship to blood, and blood often gone beserk.

Jethro's own involvements with 'blood' are not confined to the witnessing of Wilders' fight or to his own 'accident'—he is present at another blood bath that comes to involve his own initiation into 'manhood'. He is an onlooker at a ferocious encounter between

Garnet, one of the lodgers, and Vicky, the maid. She sees no reason why Jethro should 'escape' what she has to suffer. Subsequently, we are told, 'Love was supposed to smell April and May, but with Jethro for a long time afterwards, it gave off a slaughter-house stench.' The description of those journals might well be applied to Purdy's work; he is equally interested in underlining everybody's relationship to 'blood' and constantly uncovers the 'slaughter-house stench' within his characters' idealised versions of love. Jethro's journal punctures the fictions of those around him, just as his pistol shot eventually erupts into the 'loving' family tableau Elvira stage manages in celebration of her freedom. Whilst the rest of the family prefer their dream worlds, one of our last views of the forgotten son is when he lies in a barn, 'stiff as somebody dead and unclaimed in a crossroads accident'. This is the price of their freedom.

The House of the Solitary Maggot could be described as a protracted 'crossroads accident'—there is much evidence of blood having gone beserk! The *stage* that forms the continuing link between past and present in the preceding narrative is replaced by images of the *screen*. Eneas even brings down an old piano as if to accompany Nora's private showing of memories in the true fashion of the early cinema. Accordingly, the ingredients of *Jeremy's Version* are projected onto a vaster screen across which giant shadows flit in ghostly pursuit of one another, invariably colliding head-on with the wrong person at the wrong time. Many of the episodes are presented as illumined tableaux, as a series of stills, where onlookers are frozen and partitioned off from an action that is playing itself out. It is Clarence who introduces this informing image. He denies his 'blood' to the extent of assuming another name altogether to further his God-like existence in New York where he is filmed in sagas of love that Owen, for one, is disabused of. He has witnessed that act between his mother and Aiken and recognised it to be nothing more glorified than 'poking'. Clarence had played 'theatre' and 'show' as a child, his head had been filled with 'stardust' and, like Rick, he feels himself predestined for success.

Aiken is the direct opposite to Clarence; he is once described as being unable to act a part. Their antagonism marks out the battlefront of 'fiction-making' and 'reality'. The first of these

122

realms is expressed in terms of imagery connected with the blinding qualities of light. There is a deliberate punning on the words 'son' and 'sun': Clarence undergoes an apotheosis to become Sun God, he wears dressing gowns of gleaming gold. When Owen is received before the dazzling glare of the cameras, he is described as 'a much sorrier sight as he stood before his glorious actor brother than when that other bastard Phaëthon stood all but blinded before the glory of his father, Apollo'. It is as if the sun, that source of life and heat, diffuses darkness instead. The elder son has become his own 'father', the maker of his own image, and in doing so has extinguished his essential self. Thus as Clarence's public persona tightens its grip, he recedes into a state of non-being. Though he dresses like a prince, his only 'home' is a tiny room, almost nothing but a wardrobe for his motion picture clothes. His background, his accent, his name, all have been stripped away and he exists merely as a reflected image upon a cinema screen—dead as the moon, that other screen reflecting light, detached and wandering from the parent body. In the absence of his true father, Owen had idolised and hero-worshipped Clarence, as if the latter made up for the vacuum that called itself Mr Skegg. Clarence must banish Owen and the love that would demand a sacrifice of his own autonomy before he can float off into heavenly orbit to beam down memories of what he has left behind. Thus the younger brother is 'eclipsed', he is cast off into empty space and vanishes for six months into the shadows of the city's underworld. Another wanderer, he 'moons' and reflects whatever is imprinted upon his malleable self.

Whilst Owen and Clarence are 'in orbit', Aiken seems to have sprung straight out of a ploughed field! It is almost as if he were fathered by the 'blood' the other two had left behind. He is overlooked by the whole family, to begin with, a mere horse tender and paid messenger until he discovers his rightful place is elsewhere. Continually covered in the stains of the earth, not to mention manure, he epitomises man's terrestial origins. He is that 'poor, naked forked creature' with whom his family, like Lear, had to discover their essential kinship. But though he trails mud across his mother's spotless white carpets and leaves puddles of blood all over his father's floor, it is only Owen who accepts the bloodied fist that smashes through a partition 'like a gift'. The polarisation of qualities in these two brothers reformulates the characteristics of Amos and Daniel in *Eustace Chisholm and the Works*. The intersection of their destinies, that other Princes' Crossing, suggests the desperate need of bodily and spiritual qualities to break down the divisions introduced by the attitude to life their various 'parents' represent. It would seem hardly appropriate to discuss their relationship in terms of even a sublimated homosexuality. Purdy is not noticeably reticent about this or any other area of human experience. They are not presented as individuals whose love is doomed by internalised taboos or as intrinsically 'wrong', but as the two severed halves of a whole being, as hypotheses about existence.

At first, their love offers a mutual qualification of these polarities, each humanising the other as blood and spirit seek to 'know' one another, intermingling in another of the author's versions of *blutbruderschaft*. Much to the disconcertion of those around them, they re-emerge like 'twins in the womb', breathing through the 'same pair of lungs'. Aiken takes to wearing his brother's New York clothes; Owen begins to speak with the other's deep baritone voice. But as they begin to enter the human sphere, the ideal which each had identified in the other begins to break up, unleashing a flood of pain. Their 'invention' of one another and consequent declaration of independence from everybody else's 'script' brings on a new stage in the psychic warfare.

If light has been usurped as one of the instruments of a solipsistic fiction-making, so has language. Whilst Clarence perverts the former, Nora excells in the latter domain. But Aiken's story gives us a kind of cross-section of the fate of the raw materials of feeling when they are obliged to surface in mediums that have been taken over for the evasion and not the articulation of love and suffering.

The battle for words is ingeniously portrayed by the problematic recurrence of the 'whippoorwill' that hovers on the edge of the thematic pattern throughout the narrative and generates a number of ironies. It first appears when Nora suffers a momentary lapse from consciousness when Owen leaves for New York. A strange sound which can only be likened to the word 'whippoorwill' escapes her monitoring ego. Mr Skegg attaches great importance to this emanation from her suppressed self; it is a chink in her armour, a token of vulnerability which he might exploit if only he could identify the 'real' word. But as usual, Skegg can neither 'hear' nor 'see' anything of human significance. The bird, the whippoorwill, is named in imitation of the forlorn cry it utters. Thus the 'pure' sound that Nora emits, for once, is a subconscious acknowledgement of the feelings of grief and pain she deflects in her daylight world. The word recurs on another occasion, serving as an approximation of some monstrous insult hurled at Aiken by a group of men. As with Nora, though, it is associated with the receipt of acute pain. Furthermore, the component parts of the word: 'whip', 'poor', and 'will', are key concepts in the poetic texturing of the narrative. They recall Aiken's anguished cry to Owen that either he *whips* him *or* he, Aiken, *will*, and by extension, that metaphoric whiplash of life that is warded off by so many other characters as an act of will. The bird itself, flying panic-strickenly about the cage of Aiken's room at his death, or haunting the thickets as Eneas walks into the night, endorses an image of terrestial life voiced by Jeremy when he described his home as a 'prison farm for winged creatures'.

These appearances of what amount to lacunae in the web of language come, in a curious way, to constitute the very eye of the novel. Aiken himself springs from just such a gaping hole into the celluloid realm his family inhabit. Before he has learned their 'language', he moves in darkness, groping for an identity, able to express himself only in incoherent sounds and violent actions. Thus, faced with the evidence of Owen's dying eyesight, he releases 'sounds such as come from afflicted birds and animals when hunters had wounded them'. But as he forces his way into the family sphere he becomes caught up in their characteristic yearning to impose an ideal version of the world upon the real one. Owen's accelerating blindness and that other 'blind spot' in his knowledge of him—the six months' disappearance in New York—contradict his desire for a brother who is flawless and beyond the mutations of time. As he struggles desperately to preserve his ideal conceptions, Aiken is described variously as 'a trainer of some prize athlete', 'an overworked surgeon', or, on the occasion of Owen's first shave, he exhibits 'a melancholy pride as if he had created him from his own strange musings, if not from his very spittle'. 'Mr God Almighty', as Lucy calls him, goes on like a

Sutpen or even a Heathcliff, to pour his energies into wrenching recognition from the whole community by acquiring the only substance they acknowledge, money and property, in order to construct a new self which is deemed worthy of the idealised Owen. But as time demolishes his grandiose schemes, broken and humiliated, he repudiates his 'own' self, abandons Owen and marries. Instead of meeting, the two brothers cross over into the realm the other occupied. Owen rides into the night to seek out his lost love, incarnating 'sleep' and transmitting his desperate need in 'blind silence'. The 'Princes' Crossing' culminates in a series of ghastly 'accidents'; Owen falls back on the only means of expression Aiken could formerly employ—violence. His suicidal vengeance for the betrayal of love unleashes that 'slaughter-house stench' once more, forming its own commentary upon the 'painless dilemmas' Clarence minces through on his giant screen. Aiken only ever comes near to possessing his Platonic dream self during his final coma; only from the cradle of an institution does he catch 'some glimmering of another time and place when all had been one, in harmony and perfection and assured peace'. Thus he joins the swelling ranks of 'sleepers in moon-crowned valleys' and all subsequent attempts to bring him home lead only to failure and death. His estrangement from terrestial life is complete when the ghostly Owen comes to claim what is 'owing' to him. But it would seem there is no union beyond life either—the final image is that of the whippoorwill, still frantically seeking its soul-mate, in the room where Aiken lies dead.

In this manner the author creates his unique, surrealist images of human blindness. His narratives are constructed in such a way as to undermine the surface shapings of the various story-tellers. He portrays the 'colour of darkness' as the shadowy forces his characters thought to have outlawed take their inevitable toll; as 'silence' and 'blindness' creep up on the false emanations of language and light. He incorporates an underground 'grammar' by which we can read the 'titles' of the films the narrators believe themselves to be directing and starring in. Eneas tells us how, during those interruptions in Nora's narrative flood when the recording machinery broke down, 'even in those intermissions in which the eye opened suddenly and as suddenly the giant faces and "titles" vanished, one saw and heard (so it appeared to me) the

126

"silence" of the story louder and brighter than a thousand suns exploding before the eye'.

This subterranean 'grammar' is extended by the opposing image systems which are associated either with the fiction-making realm or with the darkness it has engendered. The first category comprises of images of circularity or fixity: the sun, moon, clocks, frames, spools, the eyeball itself. (The notion of circularity is implied in the very form of the narrative; the layered stages of *Jeremy's Version* are projected on to the screens and mirrors of *The House of the Solitary Maggot*.) The second variety have reference to fluids and malleable substances: blood, water, spittle, clay, mud and so on. The instruments of definition have drifted away from the raw materials of meaning. This second type of image denotes the protean possibilities of life and asserts the flux and dissolution that overtakes its arrest in any fixed shape. There is also a third category where the previous strands are interwoven in a single image: the circular lake, for example, with its hidden depths and its surface reflections of the various hues and forms of the sky. Its fusion of the various qualities of life is juxtaposed with the isolation of those qualities in another revealing mirror—the cyclone with its chaotic whirling forces of destruction, and with a still spot at its centre, one which Norma manages to occupy!

Such then is the past which so many struggle to regain in flight from what they consider to be the horrors of the present epoch. The Gilded Age to which each character turns with nostalgia turns out to be merely an earlier version of the present. The Elysian Fields is only the name of a cinema in this world. The promise of the 'family saga in the classic fireside tradition' is the cover for a very different kind of psychic history. The rapaciousness and spirit of cannibalism that is constantly associated with the present era is given its family tree in the two dynasties that are disinterred in this 'continuous novel'. On one of her rare visits to New York, Nora rails against the archetypal 'island of Manhattan with its inhuman towers and the ape-like cacaphonous speech of its deracinated inhabitants' where 'everyone who appeared before the reeling eye was selling or sold, or discarded, eaten to the husk by the steel and concrete of the machine that was the island's only soul or substance'. Her recognition of the up-dated version of the

'House of the Solitary Maggot' is expressed in the kind of out-burst Warburton was prone to. But like him, Nora does not realise the extent of her own complicity in the founding of this carnivor-ous empire.

Purdy gives us the human form of the spiritual void which he suggests has now been 'nationalised'. There is, after all, something infinitely preferable in the antics of his two families and their various audiences. They are treated with a humour that evapor-ates when the author's attention is directly focused upon mass society. Nonetheless, the venture is far from escapist, for though we might be lured into the novel by its air of exuberant fantasy and its promises of a romantic reconstruction of a lost era, our nostalgia cannot be indulged for very long. The parody of escapist art forms involves us in a very different kind of quest. At the same time, though, the author's deliberate separation of his chosen form from contemporary models reinforces his point that the values he subscribes to must necessarily seem 'out-of-fashion fiction' in the present day.

5

I am Elijah Thrush and *In a Shallow Grave*

Purdy's later work maintains its extraordinary vitality. The delicate resonances of the earliest short stories are ultimately translated into elaborate imagist canvases. He creates an original, idiosyncratic world with its own laws and language, but one which continues its ironic discourse upon the follies of the everyday societal realm we accept as reality. His novels come to advertise their divergence from the genre of literature that seeks to accommodate itself to such a society and panders to its notions of selfhood. *I am Elijah Thrush* was published between the two novels that make up *Sleepers in Moon-Crowned Valleys*, but it deserves to be considered in relation to the latest novel, *In a Shallow Grave*. Their apposition gives explicit form to the metaphysical preoccupations of the preceding body of fiction. Together, they afford a stark juxtaposition of the destruction and the discovery of authentic modes of being. In terms of the underlying pattern of the life-cycle, the particular focus of these two novels is upon the spirit's confrontation with death and with the dissolutions of time.

It is not surprising that Purdy should have been regarded as an exponent of that most contemporary revival of an older pessimism over the process of fabrication implicit in art and in language itself. At the end of *Cabot Wright Begins*, Zoe Bickle declares that she won't be a writer in a time and place like the present. In *I am Elijah Thrush* we are presented with the plight of a memorist whose attempts to engage with a particular epoch and its representative personnages collapse into nothing. Plato's mistrust of the written word has constantly been reformulated.

E

Indeed, it has become a major concern in recent American fiction, one which is authoritatively studied in Tony Tanner's *City of Words*.* But although Purdy's fascination with the relationship between language and reality is obvious, it is misleading to see him as a parodist of the processes of art. Zoe Bickle was necessarily a 'ghost writer' in his novel because her inward self had receded from the part of her that dealt in language, a phenomenon that had also effaced the human subject of her study with similar irony. Instead of portraying the writer's inevitable fictionalisation of his raw materials, Purdy develops such a regression into a metaphor of life. It is the substantial world of human relationships that is seen to be infected with fictions and its representative individual has become a 'writer', aspiring to an omniscience over others and to a transcendence of time and place more usually the prerogative of art.

I am Elijah Thrush elaborates that parallel phenomenon hinted at in *Sleepers in Moon-Crowned Valleys* where the two narrators seem to be parasitically fed upon by their subjects. In this novel the ostensible writer finds himself 'written' by his materials, and, far from fictionalising them, he is to discover that they are already pre-packaged in the form of art works. The term memoirist is exact. The life-arresting capacities of the subjects bring about the dissolution of the biographer himself; he embarks on his career as Albert Peggs, but terminates his involvement as Elijah Thrush, the very subject he was commissioned to immortalise. But Albert's failure is the vehicle of Purdy's own 'memorial' to those qualities that have been excluded from life. He does succeed in giving a 'biography', not only of a 'ghost writer' but also of the phantasmagoric world which reduces him to that status.

In terms of the American tradition, Purdy's imagination has evident affinities with writers such as Hawthorne. Their mode is one which projects the inner life into intricate symbols and archetypal patterns of experience. Whilst he also shares Hawthorne's concern for the fate of the human heart in an antagonistic culture, this is not expressed in such an unremittingly tragic view of life. In this novel the humour and wit of the surface construction co-exist with its darker tones to produce that tension of

* Tony Tanner, *City of Words: American Fiction 1950–1970* (Jonathan Cape, 1971).

130

comedy and pathos which is so peculiar to Purdy. It might seem strange to point to archetypal thematic concerns in a work which makes its initial impact by its assortment of bewilderingly baroque characters. In the first few pages we are introduced to a black memoirist and his employer, the 'antediluvian' Millicent de Frayne, an eccentric oil heiress languishing of her love for Elijah Thrush. The latter, known also as the Mime, is a poet, painter of art nouveau, the star of a private theatre and the lover ('incorrectly if not indecently') of his own great-grandson. This youth, the so-called 'Bird of Heaven', is distinguished by his muteness and unearthly beauty, not to mention his virtual imprisonment in a Dickensian 'Alimentary Foundation'. Yet beneath this idiosyncratic surface there are early intimations that we are in the presence of a highly stylised fable, one which recalls Hawthorne's fascination for Bunyan's notion that from the very gate of heaven there is a byway to the pit. Like modern versions of Ethan Brand, Purdy's characters convert men and women into puppets, reducing themselves to abstractions in the process and like Roger Chillingworth, their hearts wither as they deny that 'universal throb'.

We are alerted to the multiple levels on which the novel is to operate when Albert informs us that 'This story, neither in vocabulary or in meaning, will be in the taste of the present epoch, and for this reason as well as others I embrace it wholeheartedly.' Albert's interest in what he approvingly terms 'two "unreal" old parties' is a measure of his lack of real involvement in his own period and it suggests his predilection for seeking compensations in areas remote from it. Yet his determination not to be a writer in his particular time and place is unwittingly prophetic, for the alternative he adopts is gradually revealed to be an intensified version of what he thought to have left behind. At the same time we can detect in his statement Purdy's own ironic notion that the importance of his story will stem precisely from the way it diverges from contemporary practices. This divergence, which only masquerades as an exoticism of style and a Rabelaisian scale of character, is to be found in its satirical opposition to the 'cannibalism' which has replaced love in his own society. Thus he feels his story is unlikely to meet the requirements of popular 'taste'.

From what we learn of Albert's past, it becomes clear that other people have used him ruthlessly as the instrument of their own fantasies. One relationship he alludes to was with a 'retired liberal radical', Ted Maufritz. They had a bizarre arrangement whereby Albert was contracted to lie across a velvet couch, well protected from possible stains by goat skins and plastic covers, so as to provide a quantity of blood from one of his best veins. This was then consumed by the retired liberal radical to render himself 'worthy' of the race his donor was scion of. As other characters are to assure him, it is Albert's 'period' and he is in demand everywhere. Yet the invisibility and assassination of identity imposed on his Alabama ancestors during their enslavement has merely been replaced by a subtler variety where he is used as an anonymous ambassador of the blackness which liberal sentiments are here parodied as having deemed fashionable. Though he indulges these fantasies for financial considerations, naturally he draws little personal gratification from the type of identity such a period affords. Elsewhere he is careful to distinguish himself from the current self-assertiveness of his race. It is as if he sees their behaviour as a subordination of the individual's uniqueness to history's stereotypes, and though he concedes admiration for the violence and insurgency of his fellows, he can only use the word 'brother' in an ironic sense. He has no such feeling of belonging to an extended family. Crushed between the perverse thirsts of the white world and the spurious selfhood of his brothers, it is understandable that he should want to embrace the 'unreality' of personnages such as Millicent de Frayne and Elijah Thrush.

But Albert's past is not quite so empty as this account might suggest. He makes many veiled allusions to a 'habit' that had provided him with his only sense of a link to life. This 'habit' is an essential part of the author's analogy between Albert's adoption of Millicent and Elijah, and the period he rejected. It expresses that part of him the former world has denied—the needs of his heart had been relegated, aptly, to 'chambers' on Wall Street. Here he had secreted his only passion, a golden eagle. The feathers which are dispersed from the inner recesses of his clothing at inopportune moments in his dealings with other people have prepared us for the nature of this ultimate disclosure. Yet their materialisation in his adopted world provokes acute rage from his patrons, signifying their displeasure at such ostentatious reminders of some mysterious area of his being which contradicts the identity they would impose upon him. When Albert confides the details of his 'habit' to Elijah's great-grandson, he tells how it was the only creature ever to have trusted him and that it had been prevailed upon to draw the sustenance it needed from his own body to save it from death. He became its 'living host' and recalls how 'There was no pain like it, Bird, none under the sun, but there was no pleasure so great either, for it put me with the gods. Yes I became a spirit because of his high command.'

The terms of his confidence point to the central role accorded to Platonic doctrines in the novel's conception. The golden eagle seems to personify that immortal and ideal world glimpsed dimly through the shadows of the sensible realm. Albert's notion of being transformed into a spirit recalls Plato's metaphor of how in some eventualities lovers were capable of 'growing wings' to lift them towards the domain of perfect forms the soul was supposed to have inhabited before its incarnation. There is something ambivalent about Albert's devotion; though he keeps alive the possibility of a love that transcends self, on the other hand, if he was to be considered as a victim in the phenomenal world then he is equally so in the struggle to partake of what simulates that Platonic 'reality'. His pursuit of the love denied him elsewhere lifts him out of human involvements altogether, resulting in a literal self-sacrifice as the bird feeds rapaciously on his running blood and matter, progressively exhausting his very substance. Our first suspicions that his 'habit' might have some connection with drug addiction are not altogether irrelevant; his wasting away in the grip of an abstraction is as de-humanising eventually as Ted Maufritz's struggle to assuage his thirst for an ideal. Though Purdy recognises the attractions of that perfect love associated with the philosophy of Plato, he seeks to depict the viciousness inherent in Albert's extremity of selflessness and its antithesis of narcissism. Both are strategies which seek an escape from those constrictions of time and place, yet they succeed only in precluding meaningful relationships between individuals. The corruption of such doctrines imaged in Albert's 'habit' is mirrored in the attachment to Millicent, Elijah and that other Bird of

Heaven, which comes to replace it. Although he frequently has intuitions of the similarity of these rival attractions in his life, Albert is never able to grasp the totality of the process of self-destruction that is to issue into being.

The realm which Elijah and Millicent have constructed and to which he gains admittance seems 'heavenly'. One of Millicent's favourite pastimes is to get up early and inspect the upper regions as if they were her private preserve. Elijah is the star of the Arcturus Gardens, an apt name for what appears to be an oasis of perfections in the derelict and rotting area known as Hell's Kitchen. That the same star is also called the Bear Ward is a sly intimation that the carnivorous rumblings from Hell's Kitchen may not altogether have been excluded. Because of Millicent's munificence, Albert is able to take up residence in the exclusive Divine Fairgroves Hotel where, we are told, Father Divine himself had the 'habit' of taking his meals. When he was alive. Little wonder, then, that Albert tells us: 'I felt at times I had died and gone to the white heaven, and that Elijah and Millicent were God and Goddess there, keepers of a park, and I was their Only Son.' But though he might appear to have taken up residence in the realm of love itself, each member of this 'family' continues to pursue the Bird of Heaven in the shape of Elijah's great-grandson.

Albert's persistence in thinking that his 'real destiny' lies in his rented chambers, despite his present apotheosis, is the irony upon which the narrative movement rests. His prediction is exact, but for the wrong reasons. When at last he takes Elijah and the Bird to visit his chambers, he triumphantly throws open the star-studded door of the inner sanctuary, to reveal . . . nothing! The disclosure, which surprises only himself, confers retrospective irony on his dimly perceived connections between his employers and his secret *life*. On his earliest visit to the Arcturus Gardens, Albert had noticed that the doorkeeper of that sanctuary, Eugene Belamey, resembled nothing more convincing than 'one of those toy bridegrooms on Italian wedding cakes'. This suspicion is quickly confirmed by the master magician himself. The Mime is described as having 'no bone structure, indeed no skin, for what uttered the words was a kind of swimming agglutination of mascara, rouge, green tinting, black teeth, and hair like the plumage in a deserted crow's nest'. (One is reminded of the manuscript of the

134

luckless Bernie Gladhart in *Cabot Wright Begins*—'Indelible Smudge'.) Though solid and sweating in contrast, Albert is disturbed by a strange feeling of connection with this apparition. He tells us: 'Although white men had offered me their lust before, nobody white had ever offered me illusion, together with dream courtesy, attention and the entire backdrop of play-acting.' Elijah would seem to externalise the ingredients of Albert's inner life with which he had concocted his dream of an ideal love.

The Mime, true to his profession, has become the imitation of those qualities he desires to perpetuate in life. As an artist, his only enduring subject is himself. *He* is subsumed by his art. On one occasion he starred as 'The Most Beautiful Man in The World'. The walls of his theatre are adorned with portraits of his 'middle period', depicting him variously as 'Hiawatha, the child Moses, Apollo, and Jesus in the Garden with Mary Magdalene'. He worships all the major Greek Gods, and in his own god-like existence he appears to defy any manifestation of time's encroachment. Thus when Albert attends his first performance of the season (the number in question being 'Narcissus Drinks His Last Glass of Joy') he concedes that 'if he was ninety or seventy or a hundred, his body was as firm as an apple, and his genitals looked as hopeful as those of someone expecting to raise a large number of children'. His name, with its dual connotations of prophet and song-bird, denotes his aspirations to the ethereal sphere of Albert's golden eagle, as does his devotion to that other Bird of Heaven. But there is no qualification of his narcissism in his obsession with his great-grandson. That paragon of ideal youth and beauty is the self he covets. Though his possession of the boy is ostensibly thwarted by the 'Alimentary Foundation' within which the Bird is encaged and later by that other 'Alimentary Foundation' that calls herself Millicent de Frayne, these interventions are merely the institutionalised images of the self-imprisoning nature of his love. Like the reflection of Narcissus that stares back from the depths of the pool mouthing silently the kisses and words bestowed upon it, so the Bird is mute, effectively divorced from all human intercourse, and able only to echo the affections showered upon him in an unintelligible stream of pure sound, like that of a whole forest of singing birds. When this happens, Albert is haunted by the memory of some earlier 'half-human existence' of

his own and it comes as no surprise when he is tempted to relinquish all his other 'habits' in favour of the Bird. In this way
Purdy images the longing to escape the pain of selfhood in the
actual world and the consequences that attend life's subordination to such a dream. Thus the Mime has destroyed all inward
dimensions in the pursuit of his Bird of Heaven, and his failure
to wrest custody of his great-grandson duplicates his failure to
establish a hold over any of the god-like attributes he parodies.
Without the full complement of his props and make-up, he is
nothing. Albert has a momentary forewarning of this when, after
his employers have been *arrested*, he finds that in the cold fixity
of newsprint, their visible selves are 'inexpressibly ugly'. Similarly,
though Elijah's theatre was decked with his past triumphs, we remember that on the opposite wall hung a row of portraits of
seraphic-looking young men, the disciples who had all failed him,
his 'dead amours'. These memorialise what he continues to give
expression to—the effectual death of love, concealed beneath its
outward masks.

In his rare moments of introspection, Elijah has glimpses of the
inner vacuum he has created. He confides to Albert that it sometimes seemed as though only Millicent's eternal pursuit of him
provided any feeling of existing at all. He adds, plaintively, that
perhaps he 'was' her. Though such a surmisal may seem as improbable as Albert's 'becoming' Elijah Thrush, armed with the irony
of the Mime's prematurely triumphant cry of 'Journeys end in
lovers meeting', it is possible to retrace the intermediate stages
in this convergence of identities from which the novel derives its
formal perfections.

Like the Mime, Millicent has devoted her life to the retention
of her youth and the passion she associates with that halycon year
of 1913, namely himself. Her desire to commission a 'memoir'
of her love counterpoints Elijah's usurpation of the resources of
art to perpetuate a chosen image of himself. As Albert comes to
realise, they are in collusion to maintain the exact formula of that
'antediluvian' year. Not only does Millicent finance the Mime's
private theatre, but even their make-up and phraseology is identical. Her love has petrified to the dimensions of a 'habit', consequently her annual invasion of and expulsion from the Arcturus
Gardens is such an expected ritual that when she erupts into the

auditorium preceded by an axe-wielding young man in the garb of the Fire Department, the spectators are under no illusion that this companion is anything other than a hired accessory of her own performance. Appropriately, she is attired in an opera cloak, scarcely concealing the full suit of armour beneath. Their mutual dependence is such that it is even acted out on the stage. Millicent's appropriation of the theatre to present a selection of her own repertoire pales into insignificance when the Mime, unable to bear his exile to the wings, joins her in 'an unparalleled two-step'. As far as the audience was concerned, 'it was suddenly apparent she only needed his guiding hand to be brilliant'.

Though they have enjoined in over half a century's embalment of their youth and hypothetical 'love', Millicent does not in fact share her partner's subservience to those deities. She goes through the outward motions to suit her own purposes; telling the Bird that whilst she has known 'for nearly a hundred years there is no love under the sickly sun' she has never forbidden it even in those she was getting her best embraces from. The subordination of other people to her own monstrous appetite for power is Millicent's revenge upon the world for deluding her with its promises of love. She wants to feed upon its very substance to demonstrate her mastery over it. Although the Mime claims she is the enemy to everything that he and Albert hold dear, in fact, she is simply stripping away the sophistry with which he cloaks his own rapaciousness and thus in the deepest sense she *is* his essential self. He describes indignantly how she receives a constant stream of young men in her 'withdrawing' room and in order to preserve her youth, 'that horrible creature extracts their semen with a siphon, one extract after another from those perfect specimens of youth, without tenderness, interest in their bodies—or minds—as coldly and as calculatedly as a surgeon, dismissing them afterwards with a huge sum of money, never to see them again'. Millicent feeds upon life's own fluids in a transaction which is a grotesque parody of the release of love. But despite the Mime's cry that she is a 'monster' and shouldn't be allowed by God to rove free, she has been issued into being by such as himself, for in seeking to remove himself to a 'divine' realm he has unleashed a carnivorous demon from Hell's Kitchen.

The matriarch's exultation in her power over life is founded upon despair. The elixir Millicent extracts from her young men does not satiate her appetite even if it preserves her youth. Her sterility is spiritual. As she tells Albert when he talks confusedly about spilling his semen on the floor in front of her, she is not at all interested in what he considers to be his gift to the white world. She lusts for his soul as if the purity of that 'organ' denoted by the capacitities for suffering she has intuitively grasped could alone sustain her reign. She can listen to his weeping with 'the fine attention and critical detachment of the perfect eardrum made by God for this moment, and no other'. Millicent's fathoming of her luckless protégé's 'habit' provides her with the opportunity to consume the soul that has been secreted away from the world. Denied her being as a woman, she demonstrates the ultimate dependency of her menfolk upon her by contemptuously smashing their attempts to lift themselves out of the human sphere. They are her *creations*, and she becomes the 'writer' of their destinies as if she were the incarnation of the principle of time itself which, deprived of its spiritual dimensions, dwindles to a sardonic fatality. Albert, Elijah and both Birds of Heaven are ground to the dictates of her imperial recipe.

Albert affords the fuel upon which his employers' self-love can feed. He represents that substantial 'reality' that Millicent claimed to be located only deep under the skin. His colour and physical perfections promise an inner richness that might nourish their phantasmagorically white world. Throughout his involvement with them the excretion of his living matter is expressed metaphorically by the constant flow of sweat pouring from him as if he were the 'great punctured artery' of life itself. Albert's role as 'living host' to his eagle is duplicated in a world that masquerades as the Divine Fairgroves Hotel, but which is revealed as Hell's Kitchen with its proliferating 'soul food' restaurants. Time moves in reverse as Albert regresses to that 'half-human existence' he had glimpsed in Elijah's great-grandson. He tells us: 'Love itself was devouring me, as it returned me to a strange boyhood.' As his employers' world becomes more and more hallucinatory, he complains: 'I felt most unlike myself, although I had been getting less like myself ever since that July interview with Millicent.' Their apparent devotion is contradicted on many occasions, none more comic than when they appear to stage an

138

argument in convenient earshot from where he is spying on them from a fire escape; overwhelmed by their flattering references to his qualities of body and soul, he is moved to shed all his clothing and to offer himself up to them. Unfortunately, they are oblivious to his charms, and we learn that 'their quarrel which had been going on since 1913 could not be interrupted by a naked nigger'. In reality, he is little more than a 'poor black pawn' in their absorbing game.

The memoirist's persistence in thinking that his real destiny lies within his chambers is the cause of his final downfall. The implications of Millicent's 'great aquiline nose' are clear enough, but he cannot bring himself to believe in the 'white world' that envelops him with its talk of districts called Hell's Kitchen and its obsessions with Birds of Heaven. Ironically, the Mime is unable to credit Albert's confused confessions as to the occupant of his chambers. Their disbelief in each other's pretensions to possessing an ideal love is unwittingly prophetic, for when they examine Albert's magic sanctuary the room is empty except for a triumphal note from Millicent, their 'real' keeper. The intersection of their destinies is thus proclaimed.

Albert is a failure as a memoirist; as Millicent disparagingly retorts 'his biography does not add up to even the thinnest sliced . . . reality', an appropriate verdict, not only upon the Mime, but upon the way in which Albert is engulfed by the insubstantiality of his 'subject'. He describes his inability to come to grips with his work in revealing terms, likening the secretive notes that fall disconcertingly, as did the feathers, from the inner recesses of his clothing, to 'the droppings from immense prehistoric birds but white as the Northern snowfall'. He adds that though they were commissioned to be about Elijah Thrush, they seemed instead to be 'incoherently divergently about everything'. Albert, who began with the conviction that his adopted subject was remote from his contemporary epoch as well as his own destiny is confusedly aware that these distinctions have been broken down. As the subject of Purdy's novel, he is the medium of the exact correspondences between those seemingly distinct areas. The author plots his reduction to little more than the waste matter of the digestive systems of the prehistoric birds he refers to with great ingenuity, depicting the forces at large in the contemporary world that transform his hero's Alabama warmth to the pallid whiteness of a northern snowfall. Even Millicent has suspicions that she is a character in someone else's story, for when she comes across a sheaf of Albert's notes in the ledgers kept to refresh her memory of the exact number of the husbands she has worn out, she discovers fragments of a devastating attack, the convolutions of which grind even her thorny self to a powder.

The image systems that have reference to the rapaciousness and the soaring flight of birds converge in the final nemesis where all 'Journeys end in lovers meetings'. The Mime had commissioned a ship by the name of 'Hors de Combat' upon which to sail into the beyond, yet he finds himself for the first time in his life, according to Millicent, on the 'right' ship, the 'Queen Dick', (formerly the 'Plucked Pigeon'). Thus the Mime is obliged to submit to a union or 'marriage' with those forces he had intensified in proportion to his attempts to evade them—time, suffering and fate. He plunges into his narcissistic pool at last, and his reflected image, the Bird of Heaven, is aptly described as looking like 'a little corpse floating in the brine'. That other harbinger of divinity, Albert's eagle, is dead and stuffed, the undignified inhabitant of a glass case perched high upon a ledge to serve as the totem of the wedding feast that follows. The mounds of flowers and the smell of roasting flesh (which turns out treacherously to be the unpalatable flesh of the same beloved eagle), all suggest a funeral rite more than a marriage. The Mime feels his true age and thinks of Albert as his 'child', a metamorphosis which is ironically confirmed by the 'love letter' that is broadcast over the ocean's waves by the aid of a megaphone like a last will and testament. Since Millicent has cut him to 'mincemeat', belittled his equipment and shut him in a cabin with the ignominious title of 'News from the Past', Elijah wants his heavenly companion to keep his Platonic self alive by taking over his roles at the Arcturus Gardens. Now that his innermost self has been consumed, Albert is definitely 'equipped' to move into the 'vacancy' that has occurred. Not only has he acquired the language and the theatrical behaviour from his long exposure to such, but he can no longer remember his own name. He feels dimly that he has been present at the marriage of his own parents. His previous sensations of becoming paradoxically younger and younger now culminate in what amounts to his death and rebirth—as the mummified figure of Elijah Thrush. But even here any suggestion of choice is negated, for on his arrival back at port Eugene Belamey greets him with the words 'You received instructions didn't you . . . ,' underlining the fact that Millicent is his nemesis too. An ultimate deathlike identity has been hung on that inviting potential his former name, Albert Peggs, had anticipated.

The process of decomposition the novel addresses itself to is captured brilliantly in its formal strategies and deployment of language. The air of decadence and *fin de siècle* ornamentation of its style suggests at first a kind of literary parasitism, an affectation, even an ostentatious nostalgia for a bygone age. However, as the thematic preoccupations begin to surface, we see that the style, far from describing any fugitive impulse in its author, is the deliberate imitation of that longing to escape contemporaneity which has arrested the living development of his characters. Just as Reuben Masterson in *Eustace Chisholm and the Works* was said to be 'mucilaged' together with money, so the characters in this novel are 'mucilaged' by an ossified language that mirrors their essential stasis. Language becomes a metaphor of being and, ironically, Purdy allows us to see that their existence has no dimension other than the various 'styles' they affect as his own poetic resources 'cannibalise' their artistry to uncover the decay and decomposition within. The central image of the bird continues this dialogue with the past to reinforce the idea of the circularity of human experience. It would seem to evoke that classical Greek comedy *The Birds* by Aristophanes. Both authors transmute that desire to rise bird-like in flight from the constricting bonds of existence into a sharp satire of their contemporary societies. The Cloudcuckooland that Pisthetairos conceives of is the name applied by the Mime to Albert's chambers. Pisthetairos might well be that spirit which they felt connected them in a 'mystical real way' in a kinship thousands of years old. After all, the Mime was the 'perfect Grecian model'. Just as Pisthetairos's discontent with Athenian society and his aggressive hunger for the larger life took him into the realm of the birds where his escapism was revealed to conceal aspirations to become a God, to wear wings and to rule the world, so too, the Cloudcockooland that Albert and Elijah inhabit is overtaken and destroyed by the very tyrannies they thought to have been left behind. The characteristics of Athenian imperialism find their avatar in Millicent de Frayne as history ('that parched synthetic middling bore of a nightmare' according to its *grande dame*) describes a never ending circle. Consequently, what might appear on a cursory acquaintance to be no more than an escapist extravaganza turns out to be an ingenious and acutely perceptive fable for a time and place like the present.

Purdy's most recent novel, *In a Shallow Grave*, counterpoints this earlier work in numerous ways. If the dominant image of the previous novel was that of heaven, then this would appear to be replaced by a vision of hell. Yet their apposition is by no means ordered along the lines of Dante's dual focus, though his *Divine Comedy* might well be evoked. In each case the dominant image dissolves curiously into its antithesis. Similarly, just as the comic mode of the first is shot through with intimations of despair, so the apparent despondency of the second comes to disclose both humour and hope. The author draws upon the ancient symbols of heaven and hell to express his sense of that paradox in life whereby man has his being at the intersection of two such realms. His affinities with existential thinkers such as Kierkegaard or Unamuno illuminate this notion. In particular, the latter's *The Tragic Sense of Life* articulates a philosophy of the whole man which is close to the informing vision of Purdy's work. Unamuno's thesis that locates man's essential being in the antagonism between the soul's yearning for immortality and a timeless love, and the body's premonitions of death and dissolution, is one that Purdy might well subscribe to. His allusions to ancient doctrines and philosophies allow him to invoke the continuity of the spirit's combat with its sense of finitude, conferring irony upon his characters' imperfect glimpses of an antiquity to which they feel some dim connection. He constantly attacks dualistic conceptions of body and spirit. Each is seen to be negated when their mysterious interpenetration is denied. *I am Elijah Thrush* depicts the spirit's mutilation when it tries to wrest loose of the body's immersion in time, to annex its divine aspirations and to take up residence in a self-sufficient facsimile of that realm. The chimerical heaven dissolves into a veritable hell of non-being. Its protagonists are too *late* to comprehend the forces that ensnare and devour them, they lose the very part of themselves they sought to perpetuate. *In a Shallow Grave*, on the other hand, carries its metaphysical probings to the opposite extreme where the body's disfigurement under the shadow of death might be expected to annihilate the world of spirit. Such is not the case, however, for this last novel explores the paradox whereby a wholeness of self and an intensification of spiritual being can emerge from the depths of suffering.

In a Shallow Grave would appear to begin at the point where *I am Elijah Thrush* leaves off, the dénouement of Albert's narrative coincides, appropriately, with his own, whereas Garnet Montrose's story is only taken up after he has undergone a hideous mutilation. Condemned to a hellish world, he begins where Albert concludes, at the remotest borders of existence, as if in some purgatorial afterlife. However, just as Garnet's body has been turned inside out until it resembles some open anatomy chart, so *In a Shallow Grave* inverts the perspective of the earlier novel. It throws new light on the speech Millicent made to Albert where she insisted that 'the reality of the body is deep deep under the skin, in those parts which are ever wet, laved by the lymph and blood and running matter which is the body's only life, and all the outside, my dear, which you and I feast on, is mere death and role playing'. In her dualistic conception of body and spirit each is negated; she is neither 'at home' in her body or in the world of the spirit because of her refusal to suffer that interpenetration of the two. The consequences of such a severance are caught up in the elaborate image systems: the Bird of Heaven doubles as a Bird of Prey, and in spite of all the yearnings for a world that transcends bodily limitations, characters exist largely as the very bodies they would repudiate—though these are emptied of meaning, skin deep, surfaces to be daubed with the instruments of illusion. Relationships are reduced to transactions between bodies experienced as objects, as carrion to the taxidermist ego. But in this subsequent novel, the metaphors are reversed: the exposure of the body's very innards, the veritable geysers of blood and the lacerations of flesh, all become images of a world of spirit and are caught up within an affirmation of life.

Garnet Montrose is a veteran of the Vietnam war, though his story is not 'topical' in the sense of dealing in overt historical or political issues. Nonetheless, at a much deeper level, it examines the individual's relation to history in terms of the intersection of a personal and a collective past. The war is represented in one horrific incident which functions almost as a stark concentration of all life's power to maim and injure. Garnet was buried under the dead bodies of his comrades and all the debris of an exploding bomb, for several days. Inexplicably, he survives, though when discharged from hospital he carries the stigmata of that shallow grave all over his body like a coating of death. He describes himself as now resembling some abortion or night-goblin, stained with mulberry juice. It is as if Garnet had been stripped of every logical premise for faith in life to become the sacrificial victim of an absurd and meaningless world. Instead of coming into his inheritance as a man, he left his native Virginia at the age of seventeen to return after nine years like a macabre revenant from another age. As he tells us, 'though I was gone some nine years, I did not come back so much a man, which is what the sergeant and the captain promised us . . . I came back like somebody immemorial, drained of everything except some tiny shreds of memory. For I felt I had been gone a million years. Not only did I come back looking like somebody that was not me, but everybody close to me had left or died, the old houses were vacant about the seashore, and the young men and women were either gone or looked old and unremembering.' Thus Garnet is all alone on his tiny patrimonial estate which is like some fragment of a human map that has dissolved all around him; he is isolated if only by the fact that people scream and retch at the mere sight of him, as if suddenly confronted with their own mortality. Such an opening would seem to promise a fog of existential gloom and a paralysis of despair and yet, extraordinarily, we encounter a lyricism that encompasses both sorrow and joy and a sense of tragedy that is counterpointed by a wild humour.

When Garnet leaves hospital his pragmatic doctor warns that he must learn to forget, that his war injuries are healed and only memory holds him in pain. But memory, like the flesh on his body, has wounds which are forever reopening. It is like a shallow grave in which a dismembered hope struggles absurdly to persist and to transform itself into the present. He chooses to disregard the doctor's worldly wisdom and in lieu of the placebo of forgetfulness, he 'learns' to remember.

144

His experience supplies him with what one of his 'applicants' dubs his 'metaphysical speeches', the delivery of which reduces them to a state where, as another puts it, they would like to foam at the mouth. It is clear that not only does Garnet's corpse-like body bring people face to face with their future, but equally, he voices the constant anguish of struggling with that knowledge, an inquiry they have willed themselves to ignore. He is led endlessly to two topics he describes as simple reality to him: 'Is there any joy in the world for anybody, and has death any meaning?' The questions reformulate those that haunted the aged Nera in the play *Cracks*. Garnet's quest for some understanding of his fate has an evident religious dimension that coincides with his earthly search for some caring being. Life would appear to contradict any divine potential, or in the bitter words of a fellow soldier in the Vet's hospital, 'you can't even find anybody to shine your shoes anymore, let alone somebody to watch over you'. Whereas Garnet can picture a God, ironically He too, in the abeyance of hope, is patiently scrutinising His creation and waiting for some sign of emergent meaning. As he explains: 'my Lord you must understand I see as a kind of doglike man with a sad face Who watches the gate here, He never says anything to me, He knows my suffering, and He knows that my buddies are not as dead as I, and He knows I must walk upon the earth for a spell before going down into the total mulberry night.' Garnet's story dramatises that anxious scrutiny for meaning to be conferred on suffering and ultimate dissolution, particularising that imagined vigil by the apparently hopeless series of *interviews* he forces himself to conduct with the prospective *applicants* for that post of watching over him.

It is interesting to pursue the ramifications of these two words as they elucidate the author's overall formal strategies. 'Interviews' scarcely merit the name of such since they are cut short by a variety of perception that assimilates mere surfaces, invariably provoking retching on the part of the interviewee. As Garnet has been stripped, literally, of the outward sign of identity by which he might negotiate with a skin-deep world, he is reduced to being a monster in the eyes of others, or is possessed of a weird invisibility. This injects its own macabre humour on occasion; for example, he recounts the reaction of a party of New Yorkers in a

passing car (after he has run out of the house in pursuit of a fleeing applicant!) as, 'Where in hell are we if they are all going to
look like him now?' 'Applicants' never seem to graduate from that
provisional status; they shrink from attending his bodily needs in
the sense of applying their hands to the duties of rubbing his feet
and the skin over his heart to forestall seizures and to alleviate
distress; on another level they withdraw from touching the inner
man that is equally exposed in the letters that have to be recorded
in their own hand and delivered to the sphinx-like Widow Rance.
Words and their potential meaning fail to cohere. But this dis-
sociation is caught up in the author's larger patterning where the
same words accrue a new sense. In this instance they are brought
to discourse upon those two topics Garnet acknowledged as simple
reality to him; his situation postulates the extremity of suffering
and the inescapable facts of death towards which life's 'applicants' have to take up a stand. This might be rephrased to say
that the spirit's recoil from its body's knowledge is accentuated in
stylistic terms by those ubiquitous quotation marks that hover
around the text to denote the fracturing of a unified flow of
meaning *and* its reformation at another level. The drive to infuse
the forms of life with significance is recorded in Garnet's impas-
sioned letter writing to the chimerical personage he has named
Widow Rance. Language streams out towards the ideal it would
possess but no 'marriage' takes place. Ironically, Garnet's letters
are pure *apostrophe*, a comic invocation of the rhetorical tributes
of courtly love mixed up with his inimitable Virginian self. But
though he is marked with the gruesome insignia of a Crusader, his
Lady will not acknowledge his dedication to her service. To accept
Garnet would be to accept that she too is a 'veteran', for we learn
that not only were both her husbands lost in the same war, but
that the child she bore to each also died. Yet Garnet's skulking
behind the hollyhocks that grace her Arcadian mansion is enough
to frighten her into the grave! Therefore he is also obliged to
remain an 'applicant' and even his wildest apostrophes of love
cannot procure him an 'interview'.

This curious sense in which individual words accrue specialised
meanings is a constant feature of Purdy's work. There are many
instances in this novel other than the two that have just been
cited; similar complications arise from words like 'remember'

and 'dismember' or 'possess' and 'dispossess', to name just a few. On a more complex level, this phenomenon is duplicated in terms of narrative form. Earlier novels were seen to be organised around the dispersal of an apparent 'text' by the disclosure of others, as if the materials of the story continually shattered and reformed in the reader's mind. This was seen to give intelligible form to a collapse of being in the characters involved, or, as in the case of Alma, to the achievement of a fuller selfhood. *In a Shallow Grave* moves in a contrary direction to enact a fusion of disparate materials, assembling the shattered constituents of a human being in a process of healing. Though Garnet might seem the unlikeliest of narrators, it becomes apparent that there is something in the very nature of this paradox that imparts the author's philosophy. Time ought to be at a standstill, and yet we learn that his story dates only from the point of his premature burial. The very idea of a semi-corpse whose mind and body are almost ostentatiously in shreds, promising us a disquisition upon the meaning of life, death and what fate subsequently held in store for him, seems, to say the least, absurd. However, the voice that greets us from the opening pages and which we come to know so well, sounds unmistakeably 'human', and, to borrow a cult word, so 'together'. As with Cabot Wright's problematic beginnings, Garnet's story might be expected to communicate only a failure to begin; to be comprised of a series of interviews and applicants from which nothing ever *materialised* other than a state of being where his army nicknames 'Granite' and 'Morose' overtook and obliterated the more fanciful 'Garnet Montrose' as death completed its works. But if some of the earlier novels defined themselves by throwing doubt upon the status of their narrators, this is now comically inverted. *I am Elijah Thrush* might compose the epitaph of its own teller, but in this next instance we encounter a process of regeneration, almost a resurrection of the dead. The movement towards this formal and spiritual unity is conveyed by the workings of memory; what Garnet actually recollects is the growth of the narrative consciousness, from the point where a thought could only be momentarily committed to a scrap of paper before being burnt, to the stage where the willingness to tell his story embodied an acceptance of the mysterious commingling of joy and pain that was to await him. In brief, then, Purdy constantly dramatises the act of narration as an index of his subjects' ability to engage with their 'real life story' and as a measure of the growth or destruction of selfhood.

Whilst Garnet's 'application' for inclusion amongst the living is in abeyance, the 'coating of death' which marks him off from other people leads him to channel his hunger for spiritual sustenance towards other things that are dead or forgotten is the eyes of the world. His contemporaries feign ignorance of their temporality whereas Garnet deliberately seeks out his relation to the past. His 'bad habit' of reading is energised by the oldest and most neglected of books, just as in another sphere he cultivates a secret allegiance to the ruined dance hall that is the correlative of his own disintegration and abandonment. Garnet has absorbed the language from the ancient tomes that litter his household to the extent that his native Virginian vernacular is full of archaicisms and biblical tones. This intermixture is often comic, but on other occasions capable of a lyricism that is the perfect medium for his mystical intuitions. The interplay between the dead languages and the living is the image of the book's underlying dialogue. Furthermore, the combinatory impulse that individualises his speech can be seen as the agent of his healing process and also as the principle that governs the form of his narrative with its eclecticisms and accumulation of impressions held in the synthesis of memory. Thus Garnet browses in and rehabilitates a collective memory, renewing and being renewed by a receptivity to the past, culling fragments and scraps of knowledge that strangely soothe him. He is the first to disclaim any rational understanding of what he reads. Indeed, there is something Socratic in his professions of ignorance and his disavowal of anything pretending to objective certainty, or anything as systematised as metaphysics. The asking of questions and the pursuit of subjective, inward truths are the means by which he seeks the transcendental in life. In some ways his reading is an act of faith and a refusal to accept the finality of his own experience. Not surprisingly, the *Book of Prophecies* is a favourite work. Unamuno's declaration that it belonged to the essence of human existence to hope beyond death is echoed in Garnet's stance. His defiant hope crystallises into a premonition that some different order of applicant is at hand. Accordingly, he warns, 'I do not believe he was from this world. I believe he was sent by the Maker of All Things perhaps, if such exists.'

From the outset there are intimations that Daventry in some way incarnates this other realm that has been glimpsed in ancient books. The youth seems like an agent of the past's renewal, as if drawn inexorably to the Virginian farm by the act of faith Garnet persists in. His arrival is heralded by that of a coloured youth, Quintus Perch, himself the emissary of some softening of the world's indifference to the veteran. Quintus bears a gift of young goats and, without being asked, performs an act of kindness by removing a splinter that had become embedded in the soldier's flesh. It is significant that Daventry is first mistaken for a will o' the wisp, something motionless like a light about to go out. This suggests some fragile and homeless emanation from the world of spirit that Garnet had almost despaired of apprehending in his present plight. Furthermore, Daventry, raised on a sheep ranch in the wilds of Utah, with his 'sort of goat voice', would seem in line of descent from Pan, that other fabled shepherd and hoped for 'watcher'. Just as Pan was sometimes associated with the wind, so Daventry's fate is orchestrated by that element; initially 'quiet as a spring zephyr', the tempo steadily increases until the youth's unearthly music making is caught up within the larger movement of the hurricane.

Since Amos in *Eustace Chisholm and the Works* was also associated with Pan, it is interesting to consider the further resemblances between the two youths. Both are suddenly cast adrift in the world after the transgression of some fundamental taboo. It is as if their bodies betray them; Amos is 'exiled' by an act of incest that sprang from the concealment of his true identity, whilst Daventry, in another case of mistaken identity, abruptly finds himself the veteran of two gruesome murders, performed in *self-defence* but with the inexplicable perfection of a trained executioner. There is something almost deliberately melodramatic in the portrayal of both these events. For example, Daventry's story is like a clip from some primordial western. He is suddenly set upon behind the Ebenezer Baptist Church by two complete strangers who announce that 'The world isn't big enough for us with you in it . . .' It is as if Purdy implanted constant ironic reminders that the paradigmatic fall from grace and innocence

149

repeats itself with a now comic inevitability. Yet the mythological allusions are equally reminders that the self's divine potential is as deeply rooted as the bewilderment that occurs when its involvement in the world discloses undreamed of possibilities of evil and suffering. Exile is commuted to the search for a spiritual 'home' that will bring the self back into contact with its earliest visions. Both youths are drawn to a paternal figure who seems to promise a forgiving love and the prospect of helping them to realise some earthly identity. The fact that Daniel Hawes and Garnet Montrose are soldiers suggests a bodily as opposed to a spiritual attunement to the world. Each comes to yearn for a relation to the spiritual realm that is divined in the two youths, or rather, for a love that would reunite body and soul in a meaningful whole. It is as though both parties to the relationship were offered the hope of atonement to the part of the self that had been cast off. This is not to deny the presence of homoerotic elements and one should not misconstrue Purdy as seeking to disguise these beneath a pattern of metaphysical abstractions. On the contrary, this latter debate succeeds precisely because it is rooted in a compelling account of the feelings that develop between individuals.

Furthermore, such an analysis inevitably schematises a psychic drama which is rendered in essentially allusive terms. The author does not engage in a clumsy allegorisation, except in those instances where there is a deliberate ironic purpose. His use of literary form is at one with his vision of life as a necessary dialect of body and spirit. The amorphous, dream-like potential of youth is locked in combat with the constrictions of time. Attempts to deny this interaction have their counterpart in form. Characters may remain or regress to the abstractions of allegory, or they may move to the opposite extreme where the transcendental is repudiated and identity sought purely in terms of the material, phenomenal world. In this present novel the two extremes happily co-exist within the narrative consciousness and the story of how Garnet comes to live at such a juncture is implicit in his mode of perception. The mystical, visionary glimpses are held in synthesis with the specific and individualising detail. Thus Daventry is no 'ordinary' messenger of God and his Christ-like sacrifices are tempered by homely characteristics which are often amusing. He has no front teeth for one thing!

He differs from previous applicants in that despite the initial formality of retching, Garnet is seen for the man *he* is. And if the youth's crime was a case of mistaken identity in the additional sense that he never realised he had it *in* him to kill, Garnet, whom he describes as his 'other self', allows him to recollect that divine potential for love which he feared to have 'murdered'. Though Daventry is convinced that God will send his 'messenger' to call him to account for his crime, the veteran himself is cast in the first of such roles. Indeed, his resemblance to one of those mutilated corpses is unmistakeable! When the youth confesses his past it is 'as though a little child at last had embraced the dark goblin that has hid so long by the foot of his bed'. The image points to their mutual rehabilitation for Daventry is equally God's messenger in Garnet's eyes. He describes how, 'For the first time since I had been ruined and stained like mulberry wine, another human being had forgot how horrible I am, and was touching me and hugging me and asking for comfort'.

Yet this process of recognition unfolds at a different pace for each participant. The acquisition of knowledge operates on the very borders of consciousness, reaching out towards the language and outward signs of behaviour that have been manipulated in the cause of *self-defence*. Characters have their own version or image of events which is gradually brought into contact with some other subterranean 'story' rising from the very depths of their beings. It is like the manifestation of a fate that portends their essential inter-dependence. Resistance to this evolving pattern takes a variety of forms, but nothing can halt the force touched off by the sharing of secrets and the subsequent erosion of separate identities. Both Daventry and Quintus step outside their role as applicant, a mutiny which their patron is powerless to contain. For example, Daventry refuses to be the bearer of any more missives to the Widow, fearing some underlying scheme in the veteran's mind. But in reality, Garnet schemes to conceal his worry that Daventry, rather than the Widow, might be taken from him. Although he insists on maintaining the orthodoxy of his 'official' love and all its rituals, his inner tensions completely block his epistolatory inspiration and, for once, words fail him. In a comic reversal of role, he is obliged to have the youth dictate a letter to *him*. Whilst language pursues its circuitous route, Garnet, tells us: 'As I formed the last letter of my name, we both exchanged what was like one single same terrible look, a look like two shots which met and exploded together in the air.' With a deft irony, the medium, or rather the messenger, has become the message, and not only for Garnet, but eventually for the Widow, too.

Quintus rebels with equal irony. His official duties were two-fold; on the one hand he was to attend to Garnet's physical needs, rubbing his feet and generally aiming to keep his blood circulating, and on the other, he was to select and read materials that might 'warm' his master up to the tasks of correspondent. Yet these obligations are fulfilled with such zeal that he comes to follow Garnet around like some oracular shadow, delivering his own oblique 'messages' on the subject of his employer's follies and in particular upon his newfound 'cosiness' with the runaway. At one point Quintus warns that to be bereft of a shadow is to deliver oneself into the devil's power, to walk in the noonday sun. In terms of the novel's imagery it suggests the attenuation of being that follows on the severance of earthly connections. Quintus, like an inner voice of reason, reminds Garnet of those constrictions upon the dazzling light of a spiritual love. Just as Daventry seems to emerge from the past, so Quintus is steeped in ancient history and counters the dreams of perfection with the voice of pragmatism. He drones on interminably about the fluctuations in human fortunes, the laborious march of history and the chimera of progress, importuning the soldier with a miscellany of indigestible tracts on issues as various as the history of weather, the peregrinations of the earliest cherry trees and the nomenclature of crops. Once more we encounter the comic situation of the medium becoming the message. Garnet's applicants were to have been appendages that enabled him to pursue his courtship of his sweetheart and yet they thwart this illusion of preserving some meaning to life.

Designated roles crumble under the impact of feeling. For a while the penetration of each other's self defences is only acknowledged by indirect means. Similarly, insights into their respective situations surface in the shape of premonitions. None of them are immune to the vicissitudes of fortune. Thus when the Reverend Spinney comes to tell Quintus of his mother's death, Garnet 'knows' and can 'read' his news in advance. Whereas the face of death had scared away all Garnet's earlier applicants, he and Quintus are now able to share the emotion. The youth can only give way to his grief when he is finally alone with his friend. Though he averts his face for a moment, 'as if it still had any secret', this last barrier breaks down and he can *be himself* in the other's presence.

The novel abounds in images of the pain that accompanies this exposure of the inner self. Garnet, with his erupting and lacerated flesh, 'embodies' these notions in an obvious sense. He is amazed to discover that life's possibilities for suffering have not been exhausted. Having organised his remaining days around the conservation of love's dream, he finds that those who were to have sustained him in this illusion become the instruments of a more disturbing reality. When he is called upon to reciprocate the bond that has been cemented with Quintus by accepting that both youths have unearthed his own closely-guarded secrets, like them, he makes a last attempt to contain his vulnerability. Garnet's visits to the ruined dance-hall, like his letters to the Widow, had memorialised a past happiness. Discovery breaks the spell by which his nocturnal excursions had allowed him to re-enact the magic of the past. But anguish is matched by incredulity when Quintus goes on to tell him of the love Daventry had admitted for the soldier on the occasion they had followed him. These two strands are interwoven in his mind as he begins in a retaliatory fashion to interrogate the runaway on the lacunae in his personal history. When his roundabout enquiries come to probe the 'meaning' of the youth's declaration, Daventry cuts in with the question, 'can't I love somebody without me being put on trial for murder?' His choice of words focuses the novel's discourse upon the paradoxical combination of joy and suffering within the experience of love. It involves both the sacrifice and the acquisition of self. Garnet's movement towards this resurrection of being is observed with his endearing mixture of sentiment and humour. When Daventry prepares to leave, he tells us:

> I knew then that if I didn't get up I would never get up again, I knew then though my pride had never been so high, and my spirit so ignoble, I knew if he went I would, yes, I would die at last, and though I wanted to die I didn't want to die without him, all because mostly of that speech he had just made, no, it was all of him,

from the moment I seen him with his yellow hair and no front teeth and his sweet smile looking at me from the jungle of trees, I even liked, to tell the truth, the way he had vomited when he took me in the first time.

He was tying a bandana around his neck when I got into the room, but he never once looked at me. I went up to him several times, but he paid no more attention to me than if I was his shadow or the hollyhock bush that was looking through the window at him, I fell at his knees not because I had planned to go down on my knees before him, I was as a matter of fact passing out, and knelt to break my fall, but I knew I had to say what I had to say, for if I didn't I would be done for, so I said, *"Don't you ever leave me, Daventry".*

Yet the integrating force of emotional dependence and the acknowledgement of the bonds that have developed does not remove the subjects to some Platonic realm. Instead, their love takes the form of a submission to the mysterious interpenetration of those qualities that can be expressed variously in terms of body and spirit, mortality and the transcendental. For example, Garnet can see the youth's love as being simultaneously a heavenly benediction and a phenomenon that is governed by the earthly laws of change and dissolution. Having been soothed by the celestial music that was conjured out of his old harmonica, he tells us:

Daventry was crazy in a way you will never find in any other man. He was divine-crazy or heaven-crazy, I mean God had touched him, for instance when he said he loved me I knew what he meant, but I wanted to play the part of an ordinary soldier from Virginia and spurn him, when the truth of it was I loved him from the beginning but my deformity, my being turned inside out would not allow me at first to see he loved me for what I am. I knew then there was God, and that Daventry had been sent for me, and I knew also that he would leave me.

The notion of a divine madness recalls *The Phaedrus* where love, prophecy and the muse were seen as divine gifts that descended upon some men, allowing them to use their present experience as a means of recollecting the world of reality prior to incarnation. Purdy's outlandish veteran is the beneficiary of such gifts and his story performs, albeit in a bizarre manner, such an act of *recollection.*

The anguish that accompanies the dissolutions of time is tempered by the action of memory as it collects and unifies experience. This is hinted at in one of the fragments stored in Garnet's
consciousness from something Quintus read to him. The line 'Lilac
River, as you go to sea, bear you any news of her you took from
me?' plays like an old melody in his brain. It seems to intimate
that the transient flow of life and its process of loss might return
some whisper of hope and promise of renewal. This notion of bearing news is an iterative image, implicit in the actual momentum of
the narrative. The text comes to bristle with messages, not to
mention messengers, though their accelerating disclosures in turn
compose an encompassing mystery. The interacting forces of
'possession' and 'dispossession' continue to play out a drama that
is poetically realised and irreducible to rational formulas. On the
one hand, the world's messengers bear down on the trio with
imperious notices of change and loss. Mrs Gonzess brandishes her
pieces of paper threatening Garnet with eviction and confiscation
of his property in view of his failure to pay taxes. The Reverend
Spinney ceremoniously delivers 'the saddest news one man can
impart to another' when he informs Quintus of his mother's death.
The implacable workings of time are imaged by such tidings, but
the reminders never fail to shock. For example, at the funeral
service Garnet hears 'words I never knew or had forgot that human
beings would say to one another in public, such as we are short
in time in this life and cut down like grass, are only after all a
shadow and dust to dust and ashes to ashes . . .' Even Daventry
receives his own notice to quit when he comes across the headline
in the local paper with its cryptic warnings of hurricanes, 'like he
had found a telegram there from his sheriff'. But on the other hand,
the process of dispossession that had begun with the stripping
away of self-defences is countered by an acquisition of being that
springs from the redemptive qualities of love.

The notion of redemption surfaces dramatically in a strange
scene that forms a comic evocation of the Last Supper. Garnet and
Quintus, already bewildered by Daventry's outrage over their
failure to mention the not unknown phenomenon of hurricanes in
that locality, are spell-bound by his fierce insistence that they
both 'commune' with him. He commands them to drink the blood
that jets from his slashed chest to be mixed with the wine he has

poured into old tin farm cups. The sacrificial act with its transference of life's nutrients wards off in some mysterious way the
dispossession order that is hanging over Garnet. Daventry procures Garnet a 'home' in the world ultimately at the cost of his
own life. It would seem to image love's paradoxical purchasing
of spiritual meaning by the acceptance of mortality. Garnet unwittingly clarifies this when he muses on his words:

> "*Daventry, you are a messenger aren't you?*" I don't know why I said
> this, and I don't know what I meant when I said it. Often though
> I do say things, they come out of me, like Daventry's blood tried
> to come out from my mouth, and the words have a meaning, but
> I don't know what they signify. As Daventry said once later on
> before he left us for good, "*Garnet, you are a vessel in which is
> flowing the underground river of life*".

Though Garnet cannot objectify his sense of meaning, events
realise this discourse upon love and mortality in an intricate form.
He and Daventry forgo a suicide pact under the revolving moon of
the secret ballroom to become 'dancers in the grave', accepting
the pain of their inevitable separation and cherishing the transient
joy of *being* together. Life acrues value as they relinquish attempts
to immolate themselves from the ravages of time. Thus Daventry
goes to meet his fate in the person of the Widow Rance, his ultimate Sheriff. It is as if he now surrenders himself to time itself
in the final atonement for what he had earlier fled. Appropriately,
Georgina is at once one of those 'luscious cherries' that Quintus
had read about in his ancient history phase and the death-bringer,
the *Widow* Rance. The union with the woman is the medium of
creation and destruction. The beautiful Georgina can also don her
'hurricane cloak' to epitomise life's whirling forces of disintegration.

Garnet comes to constitute a one-man Chorus on his own submission to these forces. His utterances echo the simple poetry of
the Book of Job. For example. he tells us:

> I remember those final few days mostly by sounds. Everything was
> sound. Daventry had taught me to listen to the winds and the ocean
> again. I had paid them no more attention than my own beating heart
> and pulsing arteries. But now I listened to the ocean. I knew he was
> angry. I knew the winds were not ordinary winds either. They ran

like spirits in search of something. And the sky looked like lemon mixed with ashes. The moon was not right either. It looked like gray foam. And the birds, Daventry had wondered at their constant comment on everything from before dawn to our swift twilight. They were mostly silent, and they had lost a lot of their nests in the gales. A sandpiper was blown all the way from the ocean to our front porch, and had hurt its wings and breast, and I nursed it a while until one day it disappeared. One morning too I saw an eagle pursuing a waterbird, and both, I swear, dipped into the ocean and did not appear again.

It is as if the world around him comes alive with signs of the pursuit and consumption of the elements of life. These concluding sections of the novel are very powerful in the way they evoke the upsurge of the relentless energies composing the 'destructive element' that so fascinated Conrad. The narrative, which begins with a sense of stasis, moves with an accelerating tempo to perform its peculiar dance of celebration. The quickening undercurrents in events converge in the approaching hurricane whose Pentecostal eye singles out its chosen few. Garnet, for one, goes out to greet this deity like some crazed Kierkegaardian 'knight of faith'; although he is 'sick unto death' he has found meaning in suffering itself. In a hallucinatory scene where he encounters a weird group of religious followers with nodding countenances and nightgowns, he clings to his own Gods, embracing the feeling of insanity to declare that he loves Daventry 'like a mad child loves flame and fire'. Appropriately, in terms of the novel's underlying thesis on the possibilities of love, his healing processes are activated by a renewed disintegration. In the crucible of the storm his veins and arteries seem to move back 'inside' and his brain is now described as turning to the consistency of mulberry wine, humorously suggesting the internalising of the outer self that has brought him to a spiritual reawakening. This transformation is catalysed as the hurricane strikes, reiterating the horrendous explosion that resulted in his original disfigurement. He describes how:

The firmament parted, to judge by the sickening sound, like all God's handiwork had been throwed down by him in disgust, and the universe smashed to little bits and pieces. I saw, if I can trust to recollection, a whole forest rise and fly into the turbulence, pieces of buildings and bird feathers, clothing and earth, and sheets of water fell and then rose like the ocean had gone up to replace the heavens. There were sounds so terrible I felt my eardrums split, and where the sky had been black as a hundred midnights rushed this new heaven that was the mountain-high sea.

Daventry is claimed by the hurricane at the same moment. Georgina subsequently recounts how a freak wind singled him out, lifted him into the air and then flung him down again: 'He was mashed into that tree as though he belonged in it, you see, and his arms was stretched out as if he would enfold me.' The perfection of 'marriage' is as transient as everything else; the vision of love and the fragile body are folded back into the tree of life. It is the same spot where Garnet had his own vision of Georgina (rubbing cocoa butter into her nipples!), one that resulted in him bursting open in ecstasy all over himself before falling insensible to the foot of the tree. The manner of Daventry's death catches up all the earlier images of the craving for spiritual union in its impact with the forces of time; images of beings drawing together, sharing secrets, holding, communing and dancing, yet in the shadow of the grave.

Throughout his work Purdy explores the consequences of this craving for a quality of perfection in relationships and in life. His protagonists typically recoil from the encounter with suffering into dream worlds of their own construction. But these dream palaces decay from within. Withdrawal from the reality of other people and from the movement of time causes the suffocation of the only possibilities of being that life affords. Whereas Garnet's acceptance of the painful nature of experience effects a resurrection of these possibilities, his predecessors, for the most part, bury themselves *in a shallow grave*. Though Daventry describes Garnet and himself as 'one soul in two tormented halves', the bond of suffering created by that mutual recognition is indestructible and possessed of its own spiritual unity. The youth's choice of image underlines the author's perennial fascination with the writings of Plato. It echoes the myth recounted by Aristophanes in *The Symposium* where Zeus was imagined to have bisected the original, whole beings to punish them for their pride and their aspirations towards the status of Gods. Love was said to date from that distant epoch in that it strives to restore the ancient state by welding two beings into one and thus healing the wounds suffered by humanity.

Garnet comes to understand that the deepest love can never attain its object or arrest it from the flux of time. As he circles alone in his ruined ballroom, dreaming that Daventry might return to 'explain everything', it is Georgina who joins him instead. He remarks that 'the droll thing about getting what you long for is the longing was better, longing pains more, but it's more what you want'. He touches upon the same paradox that haunted Unamuno when he described fatality as the terrible mystery in virtue of which love dies as soon as it touches the happiness towards which it reaches out and true happiness dies with it. In this way, the continuing love for Daventry might be understood as a longing for the impossible, a longing, in fact, for God. It is a lesson that Georgina must finally learn. She awakens from her aura of self-sufficiency and begins with her own train of applicants. In an ironic reversal of roles the missives now flow from her pen in the same rhetorical style. She has embarked on the realisation of her widowhood by admitting sorrow, and thus her human name.

The cyclical form of the narrative is apt. It closes with Garnet watching and waiting once more. But it is a cycle of renewal and regeneration. The blossom is unfolding, the veteran's mulberry stain has subsided and even the ocean is subdued. It seems to Garnet that it was 'complaining, rather than angry, that it whimpered and sobbed and talked to itself in its sleep, that it digged and delved like it was looking for Daventry too'. And yet the dream of love continues to exert its antique influence. With a final flurry of messengers, the gate bangs once more and Quintus returns, like the prodigal son. He tells of a Mexican garden, fragrant with jasmine, like that fabled garden of the medieval love allegories, in which Daventry had appeared to him and urged him to reclaim the 'home' where he belonged and was needed. The healing process of recollecting the shattered fragments of love is continued by Garnet's willingness to tell his own story. It is the means by which Daventry himself is ultimately brought 'home'. By memorising and reliving his experience the veteran displays a faith that welds together all his fragmentary scraps of knowledge by trusting in the mystery of love's redemption in suffering. As he says, he is now like the man in the nursery rhyme who scratched out both his eyes in a quickset hedge and then jumped into another and scratched them back in again.

Garnet's ability to tell his own story makes him a unique figure amongst Purdy's many narrators. For once the 'writer' has a 'real-life' story to relate. He becomes the 'author' of his own existence and whereas so many of Purdy's earlier artist figures were mere ghosts, the veteran of them all comes into possession of a fully human substantiality. The fragmentation of language and reality that was dramatised by likening representative individuals to writers is finally reversed. *In a Shallow Grave* stands closest to *The Nephew* in terms of its ultimate affirmation of life's possibilities of meaning. Both Alma and Garnet undergo a spiritual awakening by a submission to the suffering involved in the deepest love. If Albert Peggs typified the process of losing one's identity and one's 'home' in language, then Garnet and Alma reinfuse words with their spiritual potency. Garnet's language, in particular, is alive with his own unique personality and at the same time with that of a collective past. It is a combination that colours the whole body of Purdy's work and constitutes his major achievement. Those human feelings that are as old as history are reformulated by an imagination that reclaims the 'languages' of the past with a wonderful originality.

Bibliography

Works

Don't Call Me by My Right Name and Other Stories (New York, William Frederick Press, 1956)

    63: Dream Palace (New York, William Frederick Press, 1956); as *63: Dream Palace: A Novella and Nine Stories* (London, Gollancz, 1957)

Color of Darkness: 11 Stories and a Novella (New York, New Directions, 1957; London, Secker and Warburg, 1961)

Malcolm (New York, Farrar Straus, 1959; London, Secker and Warburg, 1960)

The Nephew (New York, Farrar Straus, and London, Secker and Warburg, 1961)

Children is All (10 stories and 2 plays) (New York, New Directions, 1962; London, Secker and Warburg, 1963)

Cabot Wright Begins (New York, Farrar Straus, 1964; London, Secker and Warburg, 1965)

An Oyster Is a Wealthy Beast (story and poems) (Los Angeles, Black Sparrow Press, 1967)

Eustace Chisholm and the Works (New York, Farrar Straus, 1967; London, Cape, 1968)

Mr Evening: A Story and Nine Poems (Los Angeles, Black Sparrow Press, 1968)

On the Rebound: A Story and Nine Poems (Los Angeles, Black Sparrow Press, 1970)

Jeremy's Version: Part One of Sleepers in Moon-Crowned Valleys (New York, Doubleday, 1970; London, Cape, 1971)

The Running Sun (poems) (New York, Paul Waner Press, 1971)

I am Elijah Thrush (New York, Doubleday, 1972; London, Cape, 1972)

The Wedding Finger (play) (*Anthæus*, No. 10, 1973)

The House of the Solitary Maggot: Part Two of Sleepers in Moon-Crowned Valleys (New York, Doubleday, 1974)
In a Shallow Grave (New York, Arbor House, 1976)

Introductions

DAICHES, DAVID: 'A Preface to James Purdy's *Malcolm*' (*Antioch Review*, XXII: I, Spring, 1962)
LEWIS, R. W. B.: Preface to *The Nephew* (New York: Farrar, Straus and Giroux, 1967)
SITWELL, EDITH: Introduction to *Color of Darkness* (Philadelphia and New York: J. B. Lippincott and London, Secker and Warburg, 1961)
TANNER, TONY: Introduction to *Color of Darkness & Malcolm* (New York: Doubleday, 1974)

Selected Criticism

AUSTEN, ROGER: 'But for fate and ban: Homosexual Villains and Victims in the Military' (*College English*, 36:3, November, 1974, 352–9)
BALDANZA, FRANK: 'Playing House for Keeps with James Purdy' (*Contemporary Literature*, 11:4, Autumn, 1970, 488–510)
—— 'James Purdy On The Corruption Of Innocents' (*Contemporary Literature*, 15:3, Summer, 1974, 315–30)
—— 'The Parodoxes of Patronage in Purdy' (*American Literature*, 46:3, November, 1974, 347–56)
BUSH, GEORGE E.: 'James Purdy' (a checklist) (*Bulletin of Bibliography*, 28:1, January–March, 1971)
DENNISTON, CONSTANCE: 'The American Romance-Parody: a Study of Purdy's *Malcolm* and Heller's *Catch-22*' (*Emporia State Research Studies*, XIV, December, 1965, 42–59; 63–4)
FRENCH, WARREN: 'The Quaking World of James Purdy' from *Essays in Modern American Literature*, edited by Richard E. Langford (Deland, 1963, 112–22)
HERR, PAUL: 'The Small, Sad World of James Purdy' (*Chicago Review*, XIV, Autumn–Winter, 1960, 19–25)
LORCH, THOMAS: 'Purdy's *Malcolm*: A Unique Vision of Radical Emptiness' (*Wisconsin Studies in Contemporary Literature*, 6:2, Summer, 1965, 204–13)
MALIN, IRVING: *New American Gothic* (Carbondale, Southern Illinois University Press, 1962, *passim*)
MCNAMARA, EUGENE: 'The Post-Modern American Novel' (*Queen's Quarterly*, LXIX:2, Summer, 1962, 265–75)

162

NEWMAN, CHARLES: 'Beyond Omniscience' (*Triquarterly*, Fall, 1967, 37–52)

POMERANZ, REGINA: 'The Hell of Not Loving: Purdy's Modern Tragedy' (*Renascence*, XV: 2, Winter, 1963, 149–53)

SCHOTT, WEBSTER: 'James Purdy: American Dreams' (*Nation*, CXCVIII, March, 1964, 300–2)

SCHWARZCHILD, BETTINA: *The Not-Right House: Essays on James Purdy* (Columbia, Missouri Literary Frontiers, Series No. 5, University of Missouri Press, 1968)

SKERRETT, JOSEPH T.: 'James Purdy and the Works: Love and Tragedy in Five Novels' *Twentieth Century Literature*, 15: 1, April, 1969, 25–33)

TANNER, TONY: 'Frames without Pictures' Chapter Four of *City of Words* (*American Fiction 1950–1970*, London: Jonathan Cape, 1971)

WEALES, GERALD: 'No Face and No Exit: The Fiction of James Purdy and J. P. Donleavy' (*Contemporary American Novelist*, CLXXXVII, Spring, 1964, 143–54)

Interviews

'I am James Purdy' (*Andy Warhol's Interview*, December, 1972)

'James Purdy' (*Penthouse*, July, 1974)

James Purdy gives a brief personal statement on his work in *Contemporary Novelists*, edited by James Vinson (London, New York: St James Press and St Martin's Press, 1972)

Manuscript collection: Yale.

Index